Sherlock Holmes by Arthur Conan Doyle

A DRAMA IN FOUR ACTS

If ever a writer needed an introduction Arthur Conan Doyle would not be considered that man. After all, Sherlock Holmes is perhaps the foremost literary detective of any age. Add to this canon his stories of science fiction and his poems, his historical novels, his plays, his political campaigning, his efforts in establishing a Court Of Appeal and there is little room for anything else. Except he was also an exceptional writer of short stories of the horrific and macabre. Something very different from what you might expect.

Born in Arthur Conan Doyle was born on 22 May 1859 at 11 Picardy Place, Edinburgh, Scotland. From 1876 - 1881 he studied medicine at the University of Edinburgh following which he was employed as a doctor on the Greenland whaler Hope of Peterhead in 1880 and, after his graduation, as a ship's surgeon on the SS Mayumba during a voyage to the West African coast in 1881. Arriving in Portsmouth in June of that year with less than £10 (£700 today) to his name, he set up a medical practice at 1 Bush Villas in Elm Grove, Southsea. The practice was initially not very successful. While waiting for patients, Conan Doyle again began writing stories and composed his first novel The Mystery of Cloomber. Although he continued to study and practice medicine his career was now firmly set as a writer. And thereafter great works continued to pour out of him.

Index of Contents

PREMIERE HISTORY
'Sherlock Holmes', starring William Gillette.
First US performances: Buffalo, NY, October 23, 1889
First Broadway Performance: Garrick Theater, New York, November 6, 1889

CAST OF CHARACTERS (IN THE ORDER OF THEIR APPEARANCE)
Madge Larrabee
Alfred Bassick
John Forman
Billy
James Larrabee
Doctor Watson
Térèse
Jim Craigin
Mrs Faulkner

Thomas Leary
Sidney Prince
"Lightfoot" McTague
Alice Faulkner
Mrs Smeedley
Sherlock Holmes
Parsons
Professor Moriarty
Count Von Stalburg
John
Sir Edward Leighton

ACT I

DRAWING-ROOM AT THE LARRABEES. EVENING

The scene represents the drawing-room at Edelweiss Lodge, an old house, gloomy and decayed, situated in a lonely district in a little- frequented part of London.

The furniture is old and decayed, with the exception of the piano —a baby-grand. The desk is very solid. The ceiling is heavily beamed. Many places out of repair in the walls and ceilings. Carvings broken here and there.

The music stops an instant before rise of curtain. A short pause after curtain is up. Curtain rises in darkness—lights come up. MADGE LARRABEE is discovered anxiously waiting. A strikingly handsome woman, but with a somewhat hard face. Black hair. Richly dressed.

Enter FORMAN with evening paper. He is a quiet perfectly trained servant. He is met by MADGE who takes the paper from him quickly.

(FORMAN speaks always very quietly) - Pardon, ma'am, but one of the maids wishes to speak with you.

(MADGE is scanning the paper eagerly and sinks on to seat at the foot of the piano.)

MADGE - (not looking from paper) I can't spare the time now.

FORMAN - Very well, ma'am. (Turns to go.)

MADGE - (without looking up from paper) Which maid was it?

FORMAN - (turning towards MADGE again) Térèse, ma'am.

MADGE - (looking up. Very slight surprise in her tone) Térêse!

FORMAN - Yes, ma'am.

MADGE - Have you any idea what she wants?

FORMAN - Not the least, ma'am.

MADGE - She must tell you. I'm very busy, and can't see her unless I know.

FORMAN - I'll say so, ma'am.

(Turns and goes out, carefully and quietly closing the door after him —immediately coming in again and watching MADGE, who is busy with paper. Finds what she has been looking for and starts eagerly to read it. As if not seeing the print well, she leans near light and resumes reading with the greatest avidity. FORMAN quietly shuts door. He stands at the door looking at MADGE as she reads the paper. This is prolonged somewhat, so that it may be seen that he is not waiting for her to finish from mere politeness. His eyes are upon her sharply and intensely, yet he does not assume any expression otherwise. She finishes and angrily rises, casting the paper violently down on the piano. She turns and goes near the large heavy desk. Pauses there. Then turns away angrily. Sees FORMAN, calms herself at once. Just as MADGE turns, FORMAN seems to be coming into room.)

FORMAN - I could get nothing from her, ma'am. She insists that she must speak to you herself.

MADGE - Tell her to wait till to-morrow.

FORMAN - I asked her to do that, ma'am, and she said that she would not be here to-morrow.

(MADGE turns toward FORMAN with some surprise.)

MADGE - What does she mean by that?

FORMAN - Pardon me for mentioning it, ma'am, but she is a bit singular, as I take it.

MADGE - Tell her to come here—(FORMAN bows and turns to go. MADGE goes toward the piano, near where the paper lies. She sees it. Stops with hand on piano.)

Oh—Judson!

(FORMAN stops and comes down. Everything quiet, subdued, cat-like in his methods.)

How did you happen to imagine that I would be interested in this marriage announcement? (Takes up paper and sits in seat below the piano.)

FORMAN - I could 'ardly help it, ma'am.

(MADGE turns and looks hard at him an instant. FORMAN stands deferentially.)

MADGE - I suppose you have overheard certain references to the matter —between myself and my brother?

FORMAN - I 'ave, ma'am, but I would never have referred to it in the least if I did not think it might be of some importance to you ma'am to know it.

MADGE - Oh no—of no special importance! We know the parties concerned and are naturally interested in the event. Of course, you do not imagine there is anything more (She does not look at him as she says this.)

FORMAN - (not looking at MADGE—eyes front) Certainly not, ma'am. Anyway if I did imagine there was something more I'm sure you'd find it to your interest ma'am to remember my faithful services in helpin' to keep it quiet.

MADGE - (after slight pause, during which she looks steadily in front) Judson, what sort of a fool are you?

(FORMAN turns to her with feigned astonishment.)

MADGE - (Speaks with sharp, caustic utterances, almost between her teeth. Turns to him.) Do you imagine I would take a house, and bring this girl and her mother here and keep up the establishment for nearly two years without protecting myself against the chance of petty blackmail by my own servants?

FORMAN - (protestingly) Ah—ma'am—you misunderstand me —I—

MADGE - (rising—throws paper on to the piano.) I understand too well! And now I beg you to understand me. I have had a trifle of experience in the selection of my servants and can recognize certain things when I see them! It was quite evident from your behaviour you had been in something yourself and it didn't take me long to get it out of you. You are a self- confessed forger.

FORMAN - (quick movement of apprehension) No! (Apprehensive look around.) Don't speak out like that! (Recovers a little) It – it was in confidence—I told you in confidence ma'am.

MADGE - Well, I'm telling you in confidence that at the first sign of any underhand conduct on your part this little episode of yours will—

FORMAN - (hurriedly—to prevent her from speaking it) Yes, yes! I—will bear it in mind, ma'am. I will bear it in mind!

MADGE - (after a sharp look at him as if satisfying herself that he is now reduced to proper condition) Very well... Now, as to the maid —Térèse—

(FORMAN inclines head for instruction.)

Do you think of anything which might explain her assertion that she will not be here to-morrow?

FORMAN - (his eyes turned away from MADGE. Speaking in low tones, and behaviour subdued as if completely humiliated) It has occurred to me, ma'am, since you first asked me regarding the matter, that she may have taken exceptions to some occurrences which she thinks she 'as seen going on in this 'ouse.

MADGE - I'll raise her wages if I find it necessary; tell her so. If it isn't money that she wants—I'll see her myself.

FORMAN - Very well, ma'am. (He turns and goes out quietly.)

(MADGE stands motionless a moment. There is a sound of a heavy door opening and closing. MADGE gives a quick motion of listening. Hurries to look off. Enter JIM LARRABEE, through archway, in some excitement. He is a tall, heavily-built man, with a hard face. Full of determination and a strong character. He is well dressed, and attractive in some respects. A fine looking man. Dark hair and eyes, but the hard sinister look of a criminal.)

MADGE - Didn't you find him? I

LARRABEE - No. (Goes to the heavy desk and throws open the wooden doors of lower part, showing the iron and combination lock of a safe or strong- box. Gives knob a turn or two nervously, and works at it.)

(MADGE follows, watching him.)

He wasn't there! (Rises from desk.) We'll have to get a lock smith in.

MADGE - (quickly) No, no! We can't do that! It isn't safe!

LARRABEE - We've got to do something, haven't we? (Stoops down quickly before door of safe again, and nervously tries it.) I wish to God I knew a bit about these things. (Business at safe.) There's no time to waste, either! They've put Holmes on the case!

MADGE - Sherlock Holmes?

LARRABEE - Yes. (At safe, trying knob.)

MADGE - How do you know?

LARRABEE - I heard it at Leary's. They keep track of him down there, and every time he's put on something they give notice round.

MADGE - What could he do?

LARRABEE - (rises and faces her) I don't know—but he'll make some move—he never waits long! It may be any minute! (Moves about restlessly but stops when MADGE speaks.)

MADGE - Can't you think of someone else—as we can't find Sid?

LARRABEE - He may turn up yet. I left word with Billy Rounds, and he's on the hunt for him. (Between his teeth.) Oh! it's damnable. After holding on for two good years just for this and now the time comes and she's blocked us! (Goes to and looks off and up stairway. Looks at MADGE. Goes to her.) Look here! I'll just get at her for a minute. (Starting to go out.) I have an idea I can change her mind.

MADGE - (quickly) Yes—but wait, Jim.

(LARRABEE stops and turns to her.)

(She goes near him.) What's the use of hurting the girl? We've tried all that!

LARRABEE - Well, I'll try something else! (Turns and goes to archway.)

MADGE - (quick, half whisper) Jim! (LARRABEE turns, MADGE approaches him.) Remember—nothing that'll show! No marks! We might get into trouble.

LARRABEE - (going doggedly) I'll look out for that.

(LARRABEE goes out, running upstairs in haste. As MADGE looks after him with a trifle of anxiety standing in archway, enter TÉRÈSE. She is a quiet-looking French maid with a pleasant face. She stands near the door. MADGE turns into the room and sees her. Stands an instant. She seats herself in the arm-chair.)

MADGE - Come here.

(TÉRÈSE comes down a little way—with slight hesitation.)

What is it?

TÉRÈSE - Meester Judson said I vas to come.

MADGE - I told Judson to arrange with you himself.

TÉRÈSE - He could not, madame. I do not veesh longer to remain.

MADGE - What is it? You must give me some reason!

TÉRÈSE - It is zat I wish to go.

MADGE - You've been here months, and have made no complaint.

TÉRÈSE - Ah, madame—it is not so before! It is now beginning zat I do not like.

MADGE - (rising) What? What is it you do not like?

TÉRÈSE - (with some little spirit but low voice) I do not like eet, madame—eet—here—zis place— what you do—ze young lady you have up zere! I cannot remain to see! (Indicating above.) Eet ees not well! I cannot remain to see!

MADGE - You know nothing about it! The young lady is ill. She is not right here—(Touching forehead.) She is a great trouble to us, but we take every care of her, and treat her with the utmost kindness and—

(A piercing scream, as if muffled by something, heard in distant part of house above.)

(Music on scream. Very pianissimo. Agitato.)

(Pause. Both motionless. TÉRÈSE does not assume a horrified expression; she simply stands motionless. After quite a pause, MRS. FAULKNER comes down stairway rapidly, a white-haired lady, dressed in an old black gown.)

MRS FAULKNER - My child! my child! They're hurting my child!

(MRS. FAULKNER stands just within archway, looking vacantly, helplessly, at MADGE. MADGE turns, sees her and goes quickly to her.)

MADGE - (between her teeth) What are you doing here? Didn't I tell you never to come down!

(The old lady simply stares vacantly, but a vague expression of trouble is upon her face.)

Come with me! (Taking MRS. FAULKNER by the arm and drawing her towards stairs.)

(The old lady hangs back in a frightened way.)

Come, I say! (The scream again—more muffled—from above. Sudden change. Tenderly.) Don't be alarmed, dear, your poor daughter's head is bad to-day. She'll be better soon! (Turns to TÉRÈSE.) Terèse—come to me in the morning. (To old lady.) Come along, dear. (Then angrily in low threatening voice.) Do you hear me? Come!

(Takes MRS. FAULKNER off with some force up the stairs. TÉRÈSE stands looking after them. Enter FORMANquietly. He looks a moment toward where MADGE has just taken the old lady off. TÉRÈSE is looking also the same way. FORMAN goes down to TÉRÈSE. They look at one another an instant in silence. Then he speaks to her in a low voice. Just before FORMAN speaks the music stops)

FORMAN - She's made it quite satisfactory, I suppose.

(TÉRÈSE looks at FORMAN.)

You will not leave her—now?

TÉRÈSE - Leave her now? More zan evaire before! Do you hear young lady? What is eet they make to her?

FORMAN - (low voice) It may be she is ill.

TÉRÈSE - Indeed, I think it is so zat zey make her eel! I weel not remain to see! (Turning a little.) I can find another place; eet eez not so difficult.

FORMAN - Not so difficult if you know where to go!

TÉRÈSE - Ah—zhat eez it!

FORMAN - I have one address—

TÉRÈSE - (turns to him quickly) Bien—you know one?

(FORMAN nods.)

Est-ce serieux? What you call re-li-ah-ble?

FORMAN - (moves to her) Here—on this card – (Quickly takes card from pocket and pushes it into her hands.) Go to that address! Don't let anyone see it!

TÉRÈSE - (quickly looking at card while FORMAN looks away —begins slowly to read) Meester— Sheer—lock –

FORMAN - (with a quick warning exclamation and sudden turn, seizes her, covering her mouth with one hand; they stand a moment, he looks slowly round) Some one might hear you! Go to that address in the morning.

(The front door bell rings. FORMAN motions her off with quick, short motion. She goes out. FORMAN goes out to open the house door—quickly. Sound of house door opening—a solid, heavy sound—not sharp. Enter SID PRINCE, walking in quickly. He is a short, stoutish, dapper little fellow. He carries a small black satchel, wears overcoat and hat, gloves, etc., and is well dressed and jaunty. He wears diamond scarf pin, rings, etc., is quick in movements and always on the alert. FORMAN follows him on, standing near archway.)

PRINCE - (going across towards piano) Don't waste toime, you fool; tell 'em I'm 'ere, can't yer?

FORMAN - Did you wish to see Mr. Chetwood, sir, or was it Miss Chetwood?

PRINCE - (stopping and turning to FORMAN) Well, I'll be blowed! You act as if I'd never been 'ere before! 'Ow do you know but I was born in this 'ere 'ouse? Go on and tell 'em as it's Mr. Sidney Prince, Esq. (He puts satchel, which is apparently heavy, on seat at foot of piano.)

FORMAN - Oh yes, sir—I beg your pardon! I'll announce you immediate, sir. (Goes out upstairs.)

(PRINCE takes off hat, gloves, etc., laying them so as to cover the satchel. Looks about room. Walks over to the heavy desk and glances at it. Swings door of the desk open in easy business-like way.)

PRINCE - Ah! (As if he had found what he was looking for. Not an exclamation of surprise. Drops on one knee and gives the lock a turn. Rises and goes over to his satchel—which he uncovers and opens. Feels about for something.)

(MADGE and LARRABEE come downstairs and enter.PRINCE sees them, but does not stop what he is doing.)

MADGE - (going across to PRINCE) Oh, is that you, Sid? I'm so glad you've come.

LARRABEE - Hallo, Sid! ... Did you get my note?

PRINCE - (going right on with what he is doing) Well, I'm 'ere, ain't I? (Business at satchel.) ... That's what it is, I take it? (Motion of head towards desk.)

MADGE - Yes ... We're awfully glad you turned up, Sid. We might have had to get in some stranger to do it. (Going across to below piano in front of PRINCE.)

PRINCE - (standing up and looking at LARRABEE and MADGE) That would be nice now, wouldn't it? If your game 'appens to be anything off colour —!!!

LARRABEE - Oh—it isn't so specially dark.

PRINCE - That different. (Goes across to desk with tools from satchel.) I say, Larrabee—

(Quick "Sh!" from MADGE just behind him.)

LARRABEE - (at same time) Shut up!

(They look round. PRINCE looks up surprised.)

For Heaven's sake, Sid, remember—my name is Chetwood here.

PRINCE - Beg your pardon. My mistake. Old times when we was learnin' the trade together—eh!

LARRABEE - Yes, yes!

PRINCE - I 'ardly expected you'd be doin' the 'igh tone thing over 'ere, wen I first come up with you workin' the Sound Steamer Line out O' New York.

LARRABEE - Come! Don't let's go into that now.

PRINCE - Well, you needn't get so 'uffy about it! You wouldn't a' been over 'ere at all, if it 'adn't been for me ... An' youd a' never met Madge 'ere neither—and a devil of a life of it you might a' been leadin'.

LARRABEE - Yes, yes.

MADGE - We know all that, Sid—but can't you open that box for us now? We've no time to lose.

PRINCE - Open it! I should say I could! It's one o' those things it'll fall open if you let it alone long enough! I'd really like to know where you picked up such a relic as this 'ere box! It's an old timer and no mistake! (About to try some tools on lock, looks about.) All clear, you say, no danger lurking?

LARRABEE - (shaking head) Not the least!

(MADGE moves away a little, glancing cautiously about. PRINCE tries tools. LARRABEE remains near piano. Both watch him as he tries tools in the lock.)

PRINCE - (at lock) You're not robbing yourselves, I trust?

LARRABEE - (near PRINCE) It does look a little like it!

PRINCE - I knew you was on some rum lay—squatting down in this place for over a year; but I never could seem to—(business) get a line on you. (He works a moment, then crosses to get a tool out of satchel, and goes near light on piano and begins to adjust it. This must bring him where he commands stage. Stopping and looking sharply at MADGE and LARRABEE.) What do we get here? Oof, I trust?

LARRABEE - Sorry to disappoint you, but it isn't.

PRINCE - That's too bad!

MADGE - (shakes head) Only a bundle of papers, Sid.

(PRINCE works at tool an instant before speaking.)

PRINCE - Pipers!

LARRABEE - Um! (Grunt of assent.)

PRINCE - Realize, I trust?

MADGE - We can't tell—it may be something—it may be nothing.

PRINCE - Well, if it's something, I'm in it, I hope.

MADGE - Why, of course, Sid—whatever you think is due for opening the box.

PRINCE - Fair enough. (As if it was all settled to go on.) Now 'ere. (Glances round quickly.) Before we starts 'er goin' what's the general surroundin's?

LARRABEE - What's the good of wasting time on—(Going near PRINCE.)

PRINCE - (up to him) If I'm in this, I'm in it, ain't I? An' I want to know wot I'm in.

MADGE - Why don't you tell him, Jimmie?

PRINCE - If anything 'appened, 'ow'd I let the office know 'oo to look out for?

LARRABEE - Well—I'm willing to give him an idea of what it is but I won't give the name of the—(Hesitates.)

(MADGE goes up to arch.)

PRINCE - That's all I ask—wot it is. I don't want no names.

LARRABEE - (nearer PRINCE and speaking lower) You know we've been working the Continent. Pleasure places and all that.

PRINCE - So I've 'eard.

(MADGE motions them to wait. Looking off quietly. Nods them to proceed.)

LARRABEE - It was over there—Homburg was the place. We ran across a young girl who'd been havin' trouble. Sister just died. Mother seemed wrong here. (Touches forehead.)

PRINCE - Well—you run across 'er.

LARRABEE - Madge took hold and found that this sister of hers had been having some kind of love affair with a—well—with a foreign gentleman of exceedingly high rank—or at least—expectations that way.

PRINCE - A foreign gentleman?

LARRABEE - That's what I said.

PRINCE - I don't so much care about that, yer know. My lay's 'ere at home.

LARRABEE - Well, this is good enough for me.

PRINCE - 'Ow much was there to it?

LARRABEE - Promise of marriage.

PRINCE - Broke it, of course.

LARRABEE - Yes—and her heart with it. I don't know what more she expected—anyway, she did expect more. She and her child died together.

PRINCE - Oh—dead!

LARRABEE - Yes, but the case isn't; there are evidences—letters, photographs, jewellery with inscriptions that he gave her. The sister's been keeping them ... (A glance about.) We've been keeping the sister ... You see?

PRINCE - (whistles) Oh, it's the sister you've got 'ere? An' what's 'er little game?

LARRABEE - To get even.

PRINCE - Ah! To get back on 'im for the way 'e treated 'er sister?

LARRABEE - Precisely.

PRINCE - She don't want money?

LARRABEE - No.

PRINCE - An' your little game?

LARRABEE - (shrug of shoulders) Whatever there is in it.

PRINCE - These papers an' things ought to be worth a little Something!

LARRABEE - I tell you it wouldn't be safe for him to marry until he gets them out of the way! He knows it very well. But what's more, the family knows it!

PRINCE - Oh—family! ... Rich, I take it.

LARRABEE - Rich isn't quite the word. They're something else.

PRINCE - You don't mean—

(LARRABEE moves nearer PRINCE and whispers a name in his ear.)

My Gawd! Which of 'em?

LARRABEE - (shakes head) I don't tell you that.

PRINCE - Well, we are a-movin' among the swells now, ain't we? But this 'ere girl—the sister o' the one that died—'ow did you manage to get 'er into it?

MADGE - I picked her up, of course, and sympathized and consoled. I invited her to stay with me at my house in London. Jimmy came over and took this place—and when I brought her along a week later it was all ready —and a private desk safe for the letters and jewellery.

LARRABEE - (turning) Yes—combination lock and all ... Everything worked smooth until a couple of weeks ago, when we began to hear from a firm of London solicitors, some veiled proposals were made – which showed that the time was coming. They wanted the things out of the way. Suddenly all negotiations on their side stopped. The next thing for me to do was to threaten. I wanted the letters for this, but when I went to get them —I found that in some way the girl had managed to change the lock on us. The numbers were wrong—and we couldn't frighten or starve her into opening the thing.

PRINCE - Oh—I see it now. You've got the stuff in there! (Indicating safe.)

LARRABEE - That's what I'm telling you! It's in there, and we can't get it out! She's juggled the lock.

PRINCE - (going at once to safe) Oh, well, it won't take long ta rectify that triflin' error. (Stops.) But wot gets me is the w'y they broke off with their offers that way—can you make head or tail of that?

LARRABEE - Yes. (Goes nearer to PRINCE.) It's simple enough.

(PRINCE turns to him for explanation.)

They've given it up themselves, and have got in Sherlock Holmes on the case.

PRINCE - (suddenly starting) Wot's that! (Pause.) Is 'Olmes in this?

LARRABEE - That's what they told me!

MADGE - But what can he do, Sid? We haven't—

PRINCE - 'Ere, don't stand talking about that—I'll get the box open. (Goes to piano in front of LARRABEE.) You send a telegram, that's all I want! (Tears page out of his note-book and writes hurriedly The other two watch him, LARRABEE a little suspiciously. Silence for a few moments while he writes.) Where's your nearest telegraph office?

MADGE - Round the corner. (Going to above piano.)

PRINCE - (down to LARRABEE and giving him the telegram he has written) Run for it! Mind what I say—run for it.

(LARRABEE is looking at him hard.)

That's to Alf Bassick. He's Professor Moriarty's confidential man. Moriarty is king of 'em all in London. He runs everything that's shady —an' 'Olmes 'as been settin' lines all round 'im for months — and he didn't know it—an' now he's beginnin' to find out that 'Olmes is trackin' 'im down—and there's the devil to pay. 'E wants any cases 'Olmes is on—it's a dead fight between 'em! 'E'll take the case just to get at 'Olmes! 'E'll kill 'im before 'e's finished with 'im, you can lay all you've got on it.

LARRABEE - What are you telling him?

PRINCE - Nothing whatever, except I've got a job on as I wants to see 'im about in the mornin' ... Read it yourself.

(LARRABEE looks at what PRINCE has written.)

But don't take all night over it! You cawn't tell wot might 'appen. (Crosses to safe.)

MADGE - Go on, Jim!

(LARRABEE crosses, MADGE following him.)

LARRABEE - (to MADGE near archway) Keep your eyes open.

MADGE - (to LARRABEE) Don't you worry!

(LARRABEE goes out.)

(MADGE is looking after him. Quick sound of door closing. PRINCE drops down to work—real work now—at desk. Short pause. MADGE stands watching PRINCE a moment. She moves over to near piano and picks up a book carelessly, which she glances at with perfect nonchalance. After a time she speaks without taking eyes from book.)

I've heard of this Professor Moriarty.

PRINCE - If you 'aven't you must've been out in the woods.

MADGE - You say he's king of them all.

PRINCE - (working) Bloomin' Hemperor—that's wot I call 'im.

MADGE - He must be a good many different things.

PRINCE - You might see it that way if you looked around an' didn't breathe too 'ard!

MADGE - What does he do?

PRINCE - I'll tell you one thing he does! (Turns to her and rests a moment from work) He sits at 'ome—quiet and easy—an runs nearly every big operation that's on. All the clever boys are under him one way or another—an' he 'olds them in 'is 'and without moving a muscle! An' if there's a slip and the police get wind of it there ain't never any 'old on 'im. They can't touch him. And wot's more, they wouldn't want to if they could.

MADGE - Why not?

PRINCE - Because they've tried it—that's w'y—an' the men as did try it was found shortly after a-floatin' in the river—that is, if they was found at all! The moment a man's marked there ain't a street that's safe for 'im! No—nor yet an alley. (Resumes drilling.)

MADGE - (after pause) What's the idea of telling him about this? He might not want—

PRINCE - (turning to her,) I tell yer, 'e'll come into anything that gives 'im a chance at 'Olmes—he wants ter trap 'im—that's wot is an just what he'll do (Resumes work)

(PRINCE works rapidly, drill going in suddenly as if he had one hole sunk. He tries a few tools in it and quickly starts another hole with drills. MADGE starts forward at business of drill.)

MADGE - (recovering to careless) Have you got it, Sid?

PRINCE - Not yet—but I'll be there soon. (Works.) I know where I am now.

(Sound of door closing outside. Enter LARRABEE hurriedly. He is breathless from running.)

LARRABEE - Well, Sid. How goes it?

PRINCE - (working) So-so.

LARRABEE - Now about this Professor Moriarty? (Gets chair from near piano and sits behind PRINCE.)

PRINCE - (working) Ask 'er.

MADGE - It's all right, Jim. It was the proper thing to do.

(Music. Melodramatic, very pp. Hardly audible.)

(MADGE and LARRABEE move near PRINCE, looking over him eagerly. He quickly introduces small punch and hammers rapidly; sound of bolts, etc., falling inside lock as if loosened. Eagerness of all three increases with final sound of loose iron work inside lock, and PRINCE at once pulls open the iron doors. All three give a quick look within. MADGE and LARRABEE start back with subdued exclamation. PRINCE looks in more carefully, then turns to them. Pause. LARRABEE in moving back pushes chair along with him. Pause. Music stops.)

MADGE - (turning to LARRABEE) Gone!

LARRABEE - (to MADGE) She's taken 'em out.

PRINCE - (rising to his feet) What do you mean?

LARRABEE - The girl!

(MADGE stops and goes quickly to safe in front of PRINCE and dropping down feels carefully about inside. Others watch her closely. PRINCE gives back a little for her.)

(NOTE.—Their dialogue since opening of safe has dropped to low excited tones, almost whispers, as they would if it were a robbery. Force of habit in their intense excitement.)

MADGE - (rises and turns to LARRABEE) She's got them!

PRINCE - 'Ow can you tell as she 'asn't done the trick already?

LARRABEE - (quick turn on PRINCE) What's that?

PRINCE - She wants to get even, you say.

MADGE - Yes! yes!

PRINCE - Well, then, if she's got the thing out of the box there – ain't it quite likely she's sent 'em along to the girl as 'e wants to marry. (Brief pause.)

MADGE - No! She hasn't had the chance.

LARRABEE - She couldn't get them out of this room. We've Watched her too close for that.

MADGE - Wait! (Turns and looks rapidly about piano, etc.)

(LARRABEE hurriedly looks about under cushions.)

LARRABEE - Here! (Strides towards archway.) I'll get her down She'll tell us where they are or strangle for it! (Turns hurriedly) Wait here! When I get her in, don't give her time to think!

(LARRABEE goes out. PRINCE comes to the end of the piano looking off after LARRABEE.)

(Music. Very pp.)

(Brief pause. MADGE glances nervously.)

PRINCE - Wot's he goin' to do?

MADGE - There's only one thing, Sid. We've got to get it out of her or the whole two years' work is wasted.

(Muffled cry of pain from ALICE in distance. Pause.)

PRINCE - (glances off anxiously) Look 'ere, I don't so much fancy this sort of thing. (Goes to safe and collects tools.)

MADGE - Don't you worry, we'll attend to it!

(Sound of LARRABEE approaching outside and speaking angrily Nearer and nearer. Footsteps heard just before entrance. LARRABEE drags ALICE FAULKNER on, jerking her across him.)

LARRABEE (as he brings ALICE on) Now, we'll see whether you will or not! (Pause for an instant.)

(NOTE.—This scene should be played well up stage.)

(Music stops.)

(Coming down.) Now tell her what we want.

ALICE (low voice—slight shake of head) You needn't tell me, I know well enough.

MADGE - (drawing nearer to ALICE with quiet cat-like glide. Smiling) Oh no dear you don't know. It isn't anything about locks, or keys, or numbers this time. (Points slowly to the open safe.) We want to know what you've done with them!

(Pause. ALICE looks at MADGE calmly. No defiance or suffering in her expression.)

(Comes closer and speaks with set teeth.) Do you hear! We want to know what you've done with them.

ALICE - (low voice—but clear and distinct) You will not know from me.

LARRABEE - (sudden violence, yet subdued, as if not wishing servants to overhear) We will know from you—and we'll know before – (As if to cross MADGE to ALICE.)

MADGE - (motioning him) Wait, Jim! (Moves down with him a little.)

LARRABEE - (to MADGE, violently) I tell you, they're in this room —she couldn't have got them out—and I'm going to make her —(As if to seize ALICE.)

MADGE - (detaining him) No! Let me speak to her first!

(LARRABEE after an instant's sullen pause, turns and walks up stage. Watches from above sullenly. MADGE turns to ALICE again.)

Don't you think, dear, it's about time to remember that you owe us a little consideration? Wasn't it something, just a little something, that we found you friendless and ill in Homburg and befriended you?

ALICE - It was only to rob me.

MADGE - Wasn't it something that we brought you and your mother across to England with us—that we kept you here—in our own home – and supported and cared for you—

ALICE - So that you could rob me.

MADGE - My dear child—you have nothing of value. That package of letters wouldn't bring you sixpence.

ALICE - Then why do you want it? Why do you persecute me and starve me to get it? (Pause—
MADGE looking at her cruelly.) All your friendship to me and my mother was a pretence—a sham. It
was only to get what you wanted away from me when the time came.

MADGE - Why, we have no idea of such a thing!

ALICE - (turning slightly on MADGE) I don't believe you.

LARRABEE - (who has controlled himself with difficulty) Well, believe me, then.

(ALICE turns to him, frightened but calm. No forced expressions of pain and despair anywhere in the
scene.)

(Moves towards her.) You're going to tell us what you've done with that package before you leave
this room to-night!

(MADGE backs away a step or two.)

ALICE - Not if you kill me.

LARRABEE - (seizing ALICE violently by the arms or wrists at back of her) It isn't killing that's going to
do it—it's something else.

(Music melodramatic and pathetic.)

(LARRABEE gets ALICE'S arms behind her, and holds her as if wrenching or twisting them from
behind. She gives slight cry of pain. MADGE comes to her. PRINCE looks away during following—
appearing not to like the scene but not moving.)

MADGE - (sharp hard voice) Tell us where it is! Tell us and he'll stop.

LARRABEE - (a little behind—business of gripping as if wrenching her arms) Out with it!

ALICE - (suppressed cry or moan) Oh!

(NOTE.—ALICE has little expression of pain on her face. The idea is to be game.)

MADGE - Where is it?

LARRABEE - Speak quick now! I'll give you a turn next time that'll take it out of you.

MADGE - (low voice) Be careful, Jimmie!

LARRABEE - (angry) Is this any time to be careful? I tell you we've got to get it out of her—and we'll
do it too! (Business.) Will you tell? (Business.) Will you tell? (Business.) Will you –

(Loud ringing of door bell in distant part of house.)

(NOTE.—This must on no account be close at hand.)

(After bell music stops.)

PRINCE - (quick turn on ring. Short sharp whisper as he starts up) Lookout!

(All stand listening an instant. ALICE, however, heard nothing, as the pain has made her faint, though not unconscious. LARRABEEpushes ALICE into chair facing fire-place. He then hides her. MADGE goes quickly and cautiously draws picture from a small concealed window. LARRABEE stands near ALICEclose up to her. Steps heard outside. LARRABEE turns quickly, hearing steps. Make these steps distinct—slow—not loud.)

LARRABEE - (speaking off) Here!

(Enter FORMAN. He stands waiting.)

Don't go to that door; see who it is.

(FORMAN simply waits—no surprise on his face. MADGEturning and speaking in low but clear voice. LARRABEE stands so that FORMAN will not see ALICE.)

MADGE - (standing on ottoman) Tall, slim man in a long coat – soft hat—smooth face—carries ... an ebony cane – (Short, quick exclamation from PRINCE.)

PRINCE - (breaks in with quick exclamation under breath.MADGE stopped by PRINCE'S exclamation) Sherlock 'Olmes! He's 'ere!

(Pause. PRINCE quickly conceals his satchel above safe—also closing door of safe. Music melodramatic, very pp.)

LARRABEE - (moving towards piano, turns out lamp) We won't answer the bell.

PRINCE - (turning from tools, etc., and stopping him quickly) Now that won't do, ye know! Looks crooked at the start!

LARRABEE - You're right! We'll have him in—and come the easy innocent. (He turns up the lamp again.)

MADGE - There's the girl!

PRINCE - (at piano) Get her away—quick!

(ALICE is beginning to notice what goes on in a dreamy way.)

LARRABEE - Take her up the back stairway!

(MADGE takes ALICE quickly and forces her to door as they speak.)

MADGE - (stopping to speak to LARRABEE and speaking out very distinctly) She's in poor health and can't see anyone—you understand.

LARRABEE - Yes! yes! Lock her in the room—and stay by the door.

(MADGE and ALICE quickly go out. LARRABEE closes door at once and stands an instant, uncertain. Then he goes to and opens lid of box on wall seat, and gets a loaded club—an ugly looking weapon—and shoves it into PRINCE'S hand.)

You get out there! (Indicating.) Keep quiet there till he gets in the house—then come round to the front.

PRINCE - I come round to the front after 'e's in the 'ouse—that plain.

LARRABEE - Be ready for 'im when he comes out! If he's got the things in spite of us, I'll give you two sharp whistles! If you don't hear it, let him pass.

PRINCE - But if I do 'ear the two whistles—?

LARRABEE - Then let 'im have it.

(PRINCE gets off at window, which he closes at once. LARRABEE moves rapidly, kicking door of desk shut as he passes. Stands at piano, leaning on it carelessly. Turns to FORMAN.)

Go on, answer the bell.

(FORMAN bows slightly and goes. LARRABEE strolls about trying to get into an assumption of coolness. Picks up book off piano. Sound of heavy door closing outside. Brief pause. Enter SHERLOCK HOLMES, hat and stick in hand —wearing a long coat or ulster, and gloves. He lingers in the archway, apparently seeing nothing in particular, and slowly drawing off gloves. Then moves to the wall seat close at hand and sits.)

(Music stops.)

(After quite a time LARRABEE turns, throws book on piano, and saunters towards HOLMES in rather an ostentatious manner.)

Mr. Holmes, I believe.

HOLMES - (rises and turning to LARRABEE as if mildly surprised.) Yes, sir.

LARRABEE - Who did you wish to see, Mr. Holmes?

HOLMES - (looking steadily at LARRABEE an instant. Speaks very quietly) Thank you so much—I sent my card—by the butler.

LARRABEE - (stands motionless an instant—after an instant pause) Oh—very well.

(Long pause. Enter FORMAN down stairs. LARRABEE moves up near piano and turns to hear what FORMAN says.)

FORMAN - (to HOLMES) Miss Faulkner begs Mr. Holmes to excuse her. She is not well enough to see anyone this evening.

(HOLMES takes out note-book and pencil and writes a word or two on a card or leaf of the book. Tears it out of book. Pulls out watch and glances at it. Hands the card to FORMAN, taking off coat first.)

HOLMES - Hand Miss Faulkner this—and say that I have—

LARRABEE - I beg your pardon, Mr. Holmes, but it's quite useless – really.

HOLMES - Oh—I'm so sorry to hear it.

(HOLMES turns quietly to LARRABEE and looks at him. LARRABEE is a trifle affected by HOLMES' quiet scrutiny.)

LARRABEE - Yes—Miss Faulkner is—I regret to say – quite an invalid. She is unable to see anyone— her health is so poor.

HOLMES - Did it ever occur to you that she might be confined to the house too much?

(An instant's pause.)

LARRABEE - (suddenly in low threatening tone, but not too violent) How does that concern you?

HOLMES - (easily) It doesn't … I simply made the suggestion.

(The two look at one another an instant. HOLMES turns quietly to FORMAN.)

That's all. (Motions him slightly.) Go on. Take it up. (FORMANgoes out up stairway. After a moment LARRABEE turns, breaking into hearty laughter.)

LARRABEE - Ha! ha! This is really too good. (Strolling about laughing.) Why, of course he can take up your card—or your note —or whatever it is, if you wish it so much; I was only trying to save You the trouble.

HOLMES - (who has been watching him through foregoing speech) Thanks —hardly any trouble at all to send a card. (Seats himself in an easy languid way—picks up Punch.)

LARRABEE - (endeavours to be easy, careless and patronizing) Do you know, Mr. Holmes, you interest me very much.

HOLMES - (easily) Ah!

LARRABEE - Upon my word, yes! We've all heard of your wonderful methods. (Coming towards HOLMES.) Your marvellous insight—your ingenuity in picking up and following clues—an the astonishing manner in which you gain information from the most trifling details … Now, I dare say— in this brief moment or two you've discovered any number of things about me.

HOLMES - Nothing of consequence, Mr. Chetwood—I have scarcely more than asked myself why you rushed off and sent that telegram in such a frightened hurry—what possible excuse you could have had for gulping down that tumbler of raw brandy at the "Lion's Head" on the way back – why your friend with the auburn hair left so suddenly by the terrace window —and what there can possibly be about the safe in the lower part of that desk to cause you such painful anxiety.

(Pause. LARRABEE standing motionless looking at HOLMES. HOLMES picks up paper and reads.)

LARRABEE - Ha! ha! very good! Very good indeed! If those things were only true now, I'd be wonderfully impressed. It would absolutely—

(He breaks off as FORMAN enters—coming down stairs. He quietly crosses to LARRABEE, who is watching him, and extends salver with a note upon it. HOLMES is looking over paper languidly. LARRABEE takes note. FORMAN retires.)

You'll excuse me, I trust.

(HOLMES remains silent, glancing over paper and looking quietly at FORMAN. LARRABEE reads the note hastily.)

(First a second's thought after reading, as he sees that HOLMES is not observing him—then speaking.) Ah—it's from—er —Faulkner! Well really! She begs to be allowed to see—Mr. Holmes. She absolutely implores it! (HOLMES looks slowly up as though scarcely interested.) Well, I suppose I shall have to give way. (Turns to FORMAN.) Judson!

FORMAN - Sir.

LARRABEE - (emphasizing words in italics) Ask Miss Faulkner to come down to the drawing-room. Say that Mr. Holmes is waiting to see her.

FORMAN - Yes, sir. (Bows and goes out upstairs.)

LARRABEE - (trying to get on the free and easy style again) It's quite remarkable, upon my soul! May I ask—(turns toward HOLMES)—if it's not an impertinent question, what message you sent up that could have so aroused Miss Faulkner's desire to come down?

HOLMES - (looking up at LARRABEE innocently) Merely that if she wasn't down here in five minutes I'd go up.

LARRABEE - (slightly knocked) Oh, that was it!

HOLMES - Quite so. (Rises and takes his watch out.) And unless I am greatly mistaken I hear the young lady on the stairs. In which case she has a minute and a half to spare. (Moving by piano— taking opportunity to look at keys, music, etc.)

(Enter MADGE LARRABEE downstairs as if not quite strong. She has made her face pale, and steadies herself a little by columns, side of arch, furniture, etc., as she comes on, but not overdoing this. She gives the impression of a person a little weak, but endeavouring not to let it be seen.)

LARRABEE - (advancing to MADGE) Alice—or—that is, Miss Faulkner, let me introduce Mr. Sherlock Holmes.

(HOLMES is near piano. MADGE goes a step to him with extended hand. HOLMES meets MADGE and takes her hand in the utmost confidence.)

MADGE - Mr. Holmes! (Coming toward him with extended hand.)

HOLMES - (meeting MADGE) Miss Faulkner!

MADGE - I'm really most charmed to meet you—although it does look as if you had made me come down in spite of myself, doesn't it? But it isn't so at all, Mr. Holmes. I was more than anxious to come, only the doctor has forbidden me seeing anyone—but when Cousin Freddie said I might come, of course that fixed the responsibility on him, so I have a perfectly clear conscience.

HOLMES - I thank you very much for consenting to see me, Miss Faulkner, but regret that you were put to the trouble of making such a very rapid change of dress.

(MADGE slightest possible start, and recover at once.)

MADGE - Ye—yes! I did hurry a trifle, I confess. (Crosses toward LARRABEE.) Mr. Holmes is quite living up to his reputation, isn't he, Freddie?

LARRABEE - Yes … But he didn't quite live up to it a moment ago.

MADGE - Oh, didn't he! I'm so sorry. (Sits on seat at foot of piano.)

LARRABEE - No. He's been telling me the most astonishing things.

MADGE - And they weren't true?

LARRABEE - Well hardly! (HOLMES sits in arm-chair.) He wanted to know what there was about the safe in the lower part that desk that caused me such horrible anxiety! Ha! ha! ha!

MADGE - (above LARRABEE'S laugh—to HOLMES) Why, this isn't anything. (To LARRABEE.) Is there?

LARRABEE - That's just it! Ha! ha! ha! (With a quick motion swings back the doors) There's a safe there, but nothing in it.

(MADGE joins him in laughter.)

MADGE - (as she laughs) Really Mr. Holmes, that's too grotesque, ha! ha!

(HOLMES, seated in arm-chair among the cushions, regards MADGE and LARRABEE with a peculiar whimsical look.)

LARRABEE - (laughing) Perhaps you'll do better next time! (Closes safe door.)

MADGE - Yes, next time—(HOLMES is looking at them.) You might try on me, Mr. Holmes. (Looking playfully at HOLMES, greatly enjoying the lark.)

LARRABEE - Yes, what do you think of her?

HOLMES - It is very easy to discern one thing about Miss Faulkner – and that is, that she is particularly fond of the piano that her touch is exquisite, her expression wonderful, and her technique extraordinary. While she likes light music very well, she is extremely fond of some of the great masters, among whom are Chopin, Liszt. She plays a great deal indeed; I see it is her chief diversion—which makes it all the more remarkable that she has not touched the piano for three days.

(Pause.)

MADGE - (turning to LARRABEE—a trifle disconcerted by HOLMES'S last words, but nearly hiding it with success) Why that's quite surprising, isn't it?

LARRABEE - Certainly better than he did for me.

HOLMES - (rising..) I am glad to somewhat repair my shattered reputation, and as a reward, will Miss Faulkner be so good as to play me something of which I am particularly fond?

MADGE - I shall be delighted—if I can. (Looks questioningly at HOLMES.)

HOLMES - If you can! Something tells me that Chopin's Prelude Number Fifteen is at your finger ends.

MADGE - Oh yes! (Rising and forgetting her illness, and going to keyboard—crossing in front of piano) I can give you that.

HOLMES - It will please me so much.

MADGE - (stopping suddenly as she is about to sit at piano) But tell me, Mr. Holmes, how did you know so much about my playing—my expression—technique?

HOLMES - Your hands.

MADGE - And my preference for the composers you mentioned?

HOLMES - Your music-rack.

MADGE - How simple! But you said I hadn't played for three days. How did —

HOLMES - The keys.

MADGE - The keys?

HOLMES - A light layer of dust.

MADGE - Dust! Oh dear! (Quick business with handkerchief on keyboard.) I never knew Terèse to forget before. (To HOLMES.) You must think us very untidy, I'm sure.

HOLMES - Quite the reverse. I see from many things that you are not untidy in the least, and therefore I am compelled to conclude that the failure of Térêse is due to something else.

MADGE - (a little under breath—and hesitatingly—yet compelled by HOLMES' pointed statement to ask) Wh—what?

HOLMES - To some unusual excitement or disturbance that has recently taken place in this house.

MADGE - (after an instant's pause) You're doing very well, Mr. Holmes, and you deserve your Chopin. (Sits, makes preparation to play rather hurriedly in order to change the subject.)

HOLMES - Thanks.

(LARRABEE looks toward safe, far from easy in his mind, and leans on piano, giving HOLMES a glance as he turns to MADGE. MADGE strikes a few preliminary chords during above business and soon begins to play the composition spoken of. Shortly after the music begins, and while LARRABEE is looking to front or elsewhere, HOLMES reaches quietly back and pulls the bell crank. No sound of bell heard, the music supposed to make it inaudible. He then sinks into seat just at bell. After a short time FORMAN enters and stands waiting just in the archway. LARRABEE does not see FORMAN at first, but happening to turn discovers him standing there and speaks a warning word to MADGE under his breath. MADGE, hearing LARRABEE speak, looks up and sees FORMAN. She stops playing in the midst of a bar—a hesitating stop. Looks at FORMAN a moment.)

MADGE - What are you doing here, Judson?

(Brief pause because FORMAN seems surprised.)

FORMAN - I came to see what was wanted, ma'am.

(Brief pause.)

MADGE - What was wanted?

(Brief pause.)

LARRABEE - Nobody asked you to come here.

FORMAN - I beg pardon, sir. I answered the bell.

LARRABEE (becoming savage) What bell?

FORMAN - The drawing-room bell, sir.

LARRABEE (threateningly) What do you mean, you blockhead!

FORMAN - I'm quite sure it rang, sir.

LARRABEE (loud voice) Well, I tell you it did not ring!

(Pause. The LARRABEES look angrily at FORMAN.)

HOLMES - (quietly—after slight pause—clear incisive voice.) Your butler is right Mr. Chetwood—the bell did ring.

(Brief pause. LARRABEE and MADGE looking at HOLMES.)

LARRABEE - How do you know?

HOLMES - I rang it.

(MADGE rises.)

LARRABEE - (roughly) What do you want?

(HOLMES rises, takes card from case or pocket.)

HOLMES - I want to send my card to Miss Faulkner. (Gives card to FORMAN.)

(FORMAN stands apparently paralysed.)

LARRABEE - (angrily—approaching HOLMES) What right have you to ring for servants and give orders in my house?

HOLMES - (turning on LARRABEE) What right have you to prevent my cards from reaching their destination—and how does it happen that you and this woman are resorting to trickery and deceit to prevent me from seeing Alice Faulkner? (The situation is held an instant and then he turns quietly to FORMAN.) Through some trifling oversight, Judson, neither of the cards I handed you have been delivered. See that this error—does not occur again.

(FORMAN stands, apparently uncertain what to do.)

FORMAN - My orders, sir—

HOLMES - (quick—sharp) Ah! you have orders! (A sudden sharp glance at LARRABEE and back in an instant.)

FORMAN - I can't say, sir, as I—

HOLMES - (quickly breaking in) You were told not to deliver my card!

LARRABEE - (step or two up) What business is this of yours, I'd like to know?

HOLMES - I shall satisfy your curiosity on that point in a very short time.

LARRABEE - Yes—and you'll find out in a very short time that it isn't safe to meddle with me! It wouldn't be any trouble at all for me to throw you out into the street.

HOLMES - (sauntering easily towards him—shaking finger ominously) Possibly not—but trouble would swiftly follow such an experiment on your part.

LARRABEE - It's a cursed lucky thing for you I'm not armed.

HOLMES - Yes—well, when Miss Faulkner comes down you can go and arm yourself.

LARRABEE - Arm myself! I'll call the police! And what's more, I'll do it now.

(HOLMES steps down and faces LARRABEE)

HOLMES - You will not do it now. You will remain where you are until the lady I came here to see has entered this room.

LARRABEE - What makes you so sure of that?

HOLMES - (in his face) Because you will infinitely prefer to avoid an investigation of your very suspicious conduct Mr. James Larrabee—

(A sharp start from both LARRABEE and MADGE on hearing HOLMES address the former by his proper name.)

—an investigation that shall certainly take place if you or your wife presume further to interfere with my business (Turns to FORMAN.) As for you, my man—it gives me great pleasure recall the features of an old acquaintance. Your recent connection with the signing of another man's name to a small piece of paper has made your presence at Bow Street much desired. You either deliver that card to Miss Faulkner at once—or you sleep in the police station to night. It is a matter of small consequence to me which you do. (Turns and strolls near fire, picking book from mantelpiece—and sits)

(FORMAN stands motionless but torn with conflicting fears)

FORMAN - (finally in a low painful voice—whispers hoarse) Shall I go sir?

(MADGE moves to near LARRABEE, at piano.)

LARRABEE - Go on. Take up the card—it makes no difference to me.

MADGE - (quick sharp aside to LARRABEE) If she comes down can't he get them away from her?

LARRABEE - (to MADGE) If he does Sid Prince is waiting for him outside.

(FORMAN appearing to be greatly relieved, turns and goes out up stairs with HOLMES' card.)

(Pathetic music, very pp.)

(A pause—no one moves.)

(Enter ALICE FAULKNER. She comes down a little—very weak —looking at LARRABEE, then seeing HOLMES for first time.)

(Stop music.)

HOLMES - (on seeing ALICE, rises and puts book on mantel. After a brief pause, turns and comes down to LARRABEE) A short time since you displayed an acute anxiety to leave the room. Pray do not let me detain you or your wife—any longer.

(The LARRABEES do not move. After a brief pause,HOLMES shrugs shoulders slightly and goes over to ALICE. HOLMES and ALICE regard each other a moment.)

ALICE - This is Mr. Holmes?

HOLMES - Yes.

ALICE - You wished to see me?

HOLMES - Very much indeed, Miss Faulkner, but I am sorry to see – (placing chair near her)—you are far from well.

ALICE - (a step. LARRABEE gives a quick glance across at her, threateningly, and a gesture of warning, but keeping it down) Oh no —(Stops as she catches LARRABEE'S angry glance.)

HOLMES - (pausing as he is about to place chair, and looking at her) No? (Lets go of his chair.) I beg your pardon—but – (Goes to her and takes her hand delicately—looks at red marks on her wrist. Looking up at her.) What does this mean?

ALICE - (shrinking a little. Sees LARRABEE'S cruel glance) Oh —nothing.

(HOLMES looks steadily at her an instant.)

HOLMES - Nothing?

ALICE - (shaking head) No!

HOLMES - And the—(pointing lightly)—mark here on your neck. Plainly showing the clutch of a man's fingers? (Indicating a place on her neck where more marks appear.) Does that mean nothing also?

(Pause. ALICE turns slightly away without answering.)

(Looking straight before him to front.) It occurs to me that I would like to have an explanation of this ... Possibly—(turns slowly towards LARRABEE)—you can furnish one, Mr. Larrabee?

(Pause.)

LARRABEE - (doggedly) How should I know?

HOLMES - It seems to have occurred in your house.

LARRABEE - (advancing a little, becoming violently angry) What if it did? You'd better understand that it isn't healthy for you or anyone else to interfere with my business.

HOLMES - (quickly—incisively) Ah! Then it is your business. We have that much at least.

(LARRABEE stops suddenly and holds himself in.)

(Turning to ALICE.) Pray be seated, Miss Faulkner. (Placing chair as if not near enough.)

(ALICE hesitates an instant—then decides to remain standing for the present. LARRABEE stands watching and listening to interview between HOLMES and ALICE.)

ALICE - I don't know who you are, Mr. Holmes, or why you are here.

HOLMES - I shall be very glad to explain. So far as the question of my identity is concerned, you have my name and address as well as the announcement of my profession upon the card, which I observe you still hold clasped tightly in the fingers of your left hand.

(ALICE at once looks at the card in her hand.)

ALICE - (a look at him) A—detective! (Sits on ottoman, looking at HOLMES.)

HOLMES - (draws near her and sits) Quite so. And my business is this. I have been consulted as to the possibility of obtaining from you certain letters and other things which are supposed to be in your possession, and which—I need not tell you—are the source of the greatest anxiety.

ALICE - (her manner changing and no longer timid and shrinking) It is quite true I have such letters, Mr. Holmes, but it will be impossible to get them from me; others—have tried—and failed.

HOLMES - What others have or have not done, while possibly instructive in certain directions, can in no way affect my conduct, Miss Faulkner. I have come to you frankly and directly, to beg you to pity and forgive.

ALICE - There are some things, Mr. Holmes, beyond pity—beyond forgiveness.

HOLMES - But there are other things that are not. (ALICE looks at him.) I am able to assure you of the sincere penitence—the deep regret—of the one who inflicted the injury, and of his earnest desire to make—any reparation in his power.

ALICE - How can reparation be made to the dead?

HOLMES - How indeed! And for that very reason, whatever injury you yourself may be able to inflict by means of these things can be no reparation – no satisfaction—no indemnity to the one no longer here. You will be acting for the living—not the dead. For your own satisfaction, Miss Faulkner, your own gratification, your own revenge!

(ALICE starts slightly at the idea suggested and rises. Pause. HOLMES rises, moves his chair back a little, standing with his hand on it.)

ALICE - (stands a moment, very quiet low voice) I know—from this and from other things that have happened—that a—a marriage is—contemplated.

HOLMES - It is quite true.

ALICE - I cannot give up what I intend to do, Mr. Holmes. There are other things beside revenge—there is punishment. If I am not able to communicate with the family—to which this man proposes to ally himself—in time to prevent such a thing—the punishment will come later—but you may be perfectly sure it will come. (HOLMES is about to speak. She motions him not to speak.) There is nothing more to say!

(HOLMES gives a signal.)

(She looks at HOLMES an instant.) Good night, Mr. Holmes. (She turns and starts to go.)

HOLMES - But my dear Miss Faulkner, before you—

(A confused noise of shouting and terrified screams from below followed by sounds of people running up a stairway and through the halls.)

HOLMES - What's that?

(All stop and listen. Noise louder. Enter FORMAN, breathless and white. At same time smoke pours in through archway.)

FORMAN - (gasping) Mr. Chetwood! Mr. Chetwood!

MADGE and LARRABEE - What is it?

(HOLMES keeps his eyes sharply on ALICE. ALICE stands back alarmed.)

FORMAN - The lamp—in the kitchen, sir! It fell off the table —an' everything down there is blazin', sir.

MADGE - The house—is on fire! (She gives a glance towards safe, forgetting that the package is gone—but instantly recovers.)

(LARRABEE hurriedly goes out, MADGE after him. FORMAN disappears. Noise of people running downstairs, etc. ALICE, on cue "Blazin', sir," gives a scream and looks quickly at chair, at the same time making an involuntary start toward it. She stops upon seeing HOLMES and stands. Noises grow less and die away outside and below.)

HOLMES - Don't alarm yourself, Miss Faulkner—(slight shake of head)—there is no fire.

ALICE - (shows by tone that she fears something) No fire! (Stands, dreading what may come.)

HOLMES - The smoke was all arranged for by me. (Slight pause)

ALICE - Arranged for? (Looks at HOLMES.)

(HOLMES quickly moves to large upholstered chair which ALICE glanced at and made start towards a moment since.)

What does it mean, Mr. Holmes?

(HOLMES feels rapidly over chair. Rips away upholstery. ALICE attempts to stop him—but is too late, and backs to piano almost in a fainting condition. HOLMES stands erect with a package in hand.)

HOLMES - That I wanted this package of letters, Miss Faulkner.

(ALICE stands looking at HOLMES speechless—motionless – meets HOLMES' gaze for a moment, and then covers her face with her hands, and very slight motion of convulsive sob or two. HOLMES with a quick motion steps quickly in a business-like way to the seat where his coat, hat and cane are, and picks up coat, throwing it over his arm as if to go at once. As he is about to take his hat, he catches sight of ALICE'S face and stops dead where he is.)

(Music. Very pp. Scarcely audible.)

(HOLMES stands looking at her, motionless. She soon looks up at him again, brushing hand across face as if to clear away any sign of crying. The tableau of the two looking at one another is held a moment or two. HOLMES' eyes leave her face and he looks down an instant. After a moment he lays his coat, hat and cane back on seat. Pauses an instant. Turns toward her.)

HOLMES - (low voice. Brief pause) I won't take them, Miss Faulkner. (He looks down an instant. Her eyes are upon his face steadily.) As you—(still looking down)—as you—very likely conjecture, the alarm of fire was only to make you betray their hiding- place —which you did ... and I—availed myself of that betrayal —as you see. But now that I witness your great distress—I find that I cannot keep them—unless—(looking up at her) —you can possibly—change your mind and let me have them —of your own free will ... (He looks at her a moment. She shakes her head very slightly.) I hardly supposed you could. (Looks down a moment. Looks up.) I will therefore—return it to you. (Very slight pause, and he is about to start toward her as if to hand her the Package.)

(Sound of quick footsteps outside. Enter LARRABEE, with a revolver in his hand, followed by MADGE.)

(Stop music.)

LARRABEE - So! You've got them, have you? And now, I suppose we're going to see you walk out of the house with them. (Handles revolver with meaning.)

(HOLMES looks quietly at LARRABEE an instant.)

HOLMES - On the contrary, you're going to see me return them to their rightful owner.

LARRABEE - (with revolver) Yes—I think that'll be the safest thing for Mr. Sherlock Holmes to do.

(HOLMES stops dead and looks at LARRABEE and walks quietly down facing him)

HOLMES - You flatter yourself Mr. Larrabee. The reason I did not leave the house with this package of papers is not because of you, or what you may do —or say—or think—or feel! It is on account of this young lady! I care that for your cheap bravado (Looks at revolver and smiles) Really? (He looks quietly in LARRABEE'S eyes an instant, then turns and goes to ALICE.) Miss Faulkner permit me to place this in your hands (Gives her the package.)

(ALICE takes the package with sudden eagerness—then turns and keeps her eyes steadily on HOLMES)

Should you ever change your mind and be so generous, forgiving as to wish to return these letters to the one who wrote them, you have my address. In any event, rest assured there will be no more cruelty, no more persecution in this house. You are perfectly safe with your property now—for I shall so arrange that your faintest cry of distress will be heard! And if that cry is heard—it will be a very unfortunate thing for those who are responsible. Good night Miss Faulkner (Pause—turns to LARRABEE and MADGE. Coming to them) As for you sir and you, madam, I beg you to understand that you continue your persecution of that young lady at your peril

(ALICE looks at HOLMES an instant, uncertain what to do. He makes a slight motion indicating her to go. ALICE, after slight pause crosses in front of HOLMES and goes out LARRABEE makes slight move towards ALICE, but is checked by a look from HOLMES. HOLMES waits motionless eyes on ALICE until exit. Then he looks after her for a moment. Then turns and takes his coat and hat. Looks at them an instant.)

Good evening—(Walks out and the sound of heavy door closing is heard outside)

(Pause. LARRABEE and MADGE stand where HOLMES left them. Sound of window opening SID PRINCE hurries in at window.)

PRINCE - (sharp but subdued) Well! 'E didn't get it, did 'e?

(LARRABEE shakes head. PRINCE looks at him, puzzled, and then turns towards MADGE.)

Well—wot is it? Wot's the pay if 'e didn't?

MADGE - He gave it to her.

PRINCE - What!—'e found it?

(MADGE indicates "Yes" by slight movement.)

An' gave it to the girl?

(MADGE repeats slight affirmative motion.)

Well 'ere—I say! Wot are you waiting for? Now's the chance – before she 'ides it again! (Starting as if to go.)

MADGE - (stopping PRINCE) No! Wait! (Glances round nervously.)

PRINCE - Wot's the matter! (Going to LARRABEE.) Do you want to lose it?

LARRABEE - No! you're right! It's all a cursed bluff! (Starting as if to go.)

MADGE (meeting them, as if to stop them) No, no, Jim!

LARRABEE - I tell you we will! Now's our chance to get a hold of it! (Pushing her aside.)

PRINCE - Well, I should say so!

(Three knocks are heard just as PRINCE and LARRABEEreach archway. A distant sound of three heavy blows, as if struck from underneath up against the floor, reverberates through the house. All stop motionless.)

(Pause.)

(Music, melodramatic agitato, very pp. till Curtain.)

LARRABEE (in a low voice) What's that?

MADGE - Someone at the door.

LARRABEE - (low voice) No—it was on that side!

(PRINCE glances round alarmed. MADGE rings bell. Enter FORMAN All stand easily as if nothing out of the usual.)

MADGE - I think someone knocked, Judson.

(FORMAN at once goes out quietly but quickly. Sound of door outside closing again. FORMAN re-enters.)

FORMAN - I beg pardon, ma'am, there's no one at the door.

MADGE - That's all.

(FORMAN goes.)

PRINCE - (speaks almost in a whisper from above the piano) 'E's got us watched! Wot we want to do is to leave it alone an the Hemperor 'ave it!

MADGE - (low voice—taking a step or two toward PRINCE) Do you mean—Professor Moriarty?

PRINCE - That's 'oo I mean. Once let 'im get at it and 'e'll settle it with 'Ólmes pretty quick (Turns to LARRABEE). Meet me at Leary's – nine sharp—in the morning. Don't you worry a minute. I tell you the Professor'll get at 'im before to-morrow night! 'E don't wait long either! An' w'en he strikes—it means death. (He goes out at window.)

(Brief pause. After PRINCE goes MADGE looks after him. LARRABEE, with a despairing look on his face, leans on chair—looks round puzzled. His eyes meet MADGE'S as lights fade away.)

CURTAIN.

ACT II

TWO SCENES WITH A DARK CHANGE

SCENE 1

PROFESSOR MORIARTY'S UNDERGROUND OFFICE. MORNING

SCENE 1.—This scene is built inside the Second. PROFESSOR MORIARTY'S underground office. A large vault-like room, with rough masonry walls and vaulted ceiling. The general idea of this place is that it has been converted from a cellar room of a warehouse into a fairly comfortable office or head-quarters. There are no windows.

The colour or tone of this set must not be similar to the third Act set, which is a gloomy and dark bluish-brown. The effect in this set should be of masonry that has long ago been whitewashed and is now old, stained and grimy. Maps on wall of England, France, Germany, Russia, etc. Also a marked map of London—heavy spots upon certain localities. Many charts of buildings, plans of floors—possible tunnellings, etc. Many books about—on impoverished shelves, etc.

PROFESSOR ROBERT MORIARTY is seated at a large circular desk facing the front. He is looking over letters, telegrams, papers, etc., as if morning mail. He is a middle-aged man, with massive head and grey hair, and a face full of character, overhanging brow, heavy jaw. A man of great intellectual force, extremely tall and thin. His forehead domes out in a white curve, and his two eyes are deeply sunken in his head. Clean-shaven, pale, ascetic-looking. Shoulders rounded, and face protruding forward, and for ever oscillating from side to side in a curiously reptilian fashion. Deep hollow voice.

The room is dark, with light showing on his face, as if from lamp. Pause. MORIARTY rings a gong at desk, which has a Peculiar sound. In a second, buzzer outside door replies twice. He Picks up a speaking tube and puts it to his mouth.

MORIARTY - (speaking into tube in a low voice) Number. (He Places tube to his ear and listens, then speaks into it again.)Correct. (Drops tube. He moves a lever up against wall and the bolt of the door slides back with a solid heavy sound.)

(Enter JOHN noiselessly. No sound of steps. He stands just within the door in the half darkness.)

Has any report come in from Chibley?

JOHN - Nothing yet sir.

MORIARTY - All the others are heard from?

JOHN - Yes, sir.

MORIARTY - I was afraid we'd have trouble there. If anything happened we lose Hickson—one of our best men. Send Bassick.

(JOHN goes out. Bolt slides back. Buzzer outside door rings twice. MORIARTY picks up tube and speaks into it)

(Speaking into tube.) Number. (Listens. Speaks into tube again.) Correct. (He slides back bolt of door.)

(Enter BASSICK noiselessly Bolt of door slides back. BASSICK goes to MORIARTY'S desk at once and stands. MORIARTY motions to sit. He does so)

Before we go into anything else, I want to refer to Davidson.

BASSICK - I've made a note of him myself, sir; he's holding bad money.

MORIARTY - Something like six hundred short on that last haul, isn't it?

BASSICK - Certainly as much as that.

MORIARTY - Have him attended to. Craigin is the one to do it. (BASSICK writes a memo quickly) And see that his disappearance is noticed. Have it spoken of. That finishes Davidson … Now as to this Blaisdell matter —did you learn anything more?

BASSICK - The whole thing was a trap.

MORIARTY - What do you mean?

BASSICK - Set and baited by an expert.

MORIARTY - But those letters and papers of instructions—you brought them back, or destroyed them, I trust?

BASSICK - I could not do it, sir—Manning has disappeared and the papers are gone!

(Music melodramatic. Cue, as MORIARTY looks at BASSICK.)

MORIARTY - Gone! Sherlock Holmes again. That's bad for the Underwood trial.

BASSICK - I thought Shackleford was going to get a postponement.

MORIARTY - He tried to—and found he was blocked.

BASSICK - Who could have done it?

(MORIARTY turns and looks at BASSICK almost hypnotically—his head vibrating from side to side as if making him speak the name.)

Sherlock Holmes?

MORIARTY - Sherlock Holmes again. (His eyes still on BASSICK.)

BASSICK - (as if fascinated by MORIARTY. Slight affirmative motion.) He's got hold of between twenty and thirty papers and instructions in as many different jobs, and some as to putting a man or two out of the way – and he's gradually completing chains of evidence which, if we let him go on, will reach to me as sure as the sun will rise. Reach to me!—Ha! (Sneer.) He's playing rather a dangerous game! Inspector Wilson tried it seven years ago. Wilson is dead. Two years later Henderson took it up. We haven't heard anything of Henderson lately, eh?

BASSICK - (shaking head) Not a thing, sir.

MORIARTY - Ha! (Sneer.) This Holmes is rather a talented man. He hopes to drag me in at the Underwood trial, but he doesn't realize what can happen between now and Monday. He doesn't know that there isn't a street in London that'll be safe for him if I whisper his name to Craigin—I might even make him a little call myself—just for the satisfaction of it—(business of head swaying, etc.)—just for the satisfaction of it. (BASSICK watches MORIARTY with some anxiety.) Baker Street, isn't it? His place—Baker Street—eh?

BASSICK - Baker Street, sir.

MORIARTY - We could make it safe. We could make it absolutely secure for three streets each way.

BASSICK - Yes, sir, but—

MORIARTY - We could. We've done it over and over again elsewhere – Police decoyed. Men in every doorway. (Sudden turn to him.) Do this to- night—in Baker Street! At nine o'clock call his attendants out on one pretext and another, and keep them out—you understand! I'll see this Sherlock Holmes myself—I'll give him a chance for his life. If he declines to treat with me—

(He takes a savage-looking bulldog revolver from under desk and examines it carefully, slowly placing it in breast pocket. Ring of telephone bell is heard, but not until the revolver business is finished.)

(The music stops.)

(MORIARTY gives a nod to BASSICK, indicating him to attend to phone. BASSICK rises and goes to and picks up telephone. MORIARTY resumes business of examining papers on his desk.)

BASSICK - (speaks into receiver and listens as indicated) Yes —yes—Bassick—What name did you say? Oh, Prince, yes. He'll have to wait—Yes—I got his telegram last night – Well, tell him to come and speak to me at the phone. (Longer wait.) Yes—I got your telegram, Prince, but I have an important matter on. You'll have to wait—Who? (Suddenly becomes very interested.) What sort of a game is it?—Where is he now?—Wait a moment. (To MORIARTY.) Here's something, sir. Sid Prince has come here over some job, and he says he's got Holmes fighting against him.

MORIARTY - (quickly turning to BASSICK) Eh? Ask him what it is. Ask him what it is. (BASSICK is about to speak through the telephone. Quickly.) Wait! (BASSICK stops.) Let him come here. (BASSICK turns in surprise.)

BASSICK - No one sees you—no one knows you. That has meant safety for years.

MORIARTY - No one sees me now. You talk with him—I'll listen from the next room. (BASSICK looks at him hesitatingly an instant.) This is your office—you understand—your office—I'll be there.

(BASSICK turns to telephone.)

BASSICK - (speaking into telephone) Is that you, Prince? – Yes, I find I can't come out—but I'll see you here—What interest have they got? What's the name? (Listening a moment. Looks round to MORIARTY.) He says there's two with him—a man and a woman named Larrabee. They won't consent to any interview unless they're present.

MORIARTY - Send them in.

BASSICK - (speaking into telephone) Eh, Prince—ask Beads to come to the telephone—Beads—eh—? (Lower voice.) Those people with Prince, do they seem to be all right? Look close yes?—Well—take them out through the warehouse and down by the circular stairway and then bring them up here by the long tunnel —Yes, here—Look them over as you go along to see they're not carrying anything—and watch that no one sees you come down – Yes—(Hangs up ear-piece, turns and looks at MORIARTY.) I don't like this, sir!

MORIARTY - (rises) You don't like this! You don't like this! I tell you it's certain death unless we can settle with this man Holmes.

(The buzzer rings three times.)

(Moves towards opening.) Your office, you understand—your office.

(BASSICK looks at MORIARTY. MORIARTY goes out. BASSICK, after MORIARTY is well off, goes and takes MORIARTY'S place at the back of the desk. Rings gong at desk. Buzzer replies twice from outside.)

BASSICK - (speaking into tube) Send John here.

(BASSICK pushes back bolt. Enter JOHN noiselessly. He stands just within door. Bolt of door slides back when door shuts.)

There are some people coming in here, you stand over there, and keep your eye on them from behind. If you see anything suspicious, drop your handkerchief. If it's the woman pick it up—if it's the man leave it on the floor.

(Three knocks are distinctly heard on door from outside. On last knock JOHN goes near wall.)

(Picks up tube and speaks into it.) Number. (Listens – speaking into tube.) Are the three waiting with you? (Listens – drops tube and pushes lever back, and the bolt slides back from the door. The door slowly swings open.)

(Enter SID PRINCE, followed by MADGE and LARRABEE. The door Closes and the bolts slide back with a clang. At the sound of the bolts LARRABEE looks round at door very sharply, realizing that they are all locked in. BASSICK motions MADGE to chair. MADGE Sits. LARRABEE is suspicious, and does not like the look of the place. PRINCE remains standing. BASSICK sits behind desk. JOHN is in the dark, watching LARRABEE and MADGE, with a handkerchief in hand.)

I understand you to say—through our private telephone—that you've got something with Sherlock Holmes against you.

PRINCE - Yes, sir—we 'ave.

BASSICK - Kindly let me have the particulars.

(LARRABEE gives "H'm," indicating that he wants to hear.)

PRINCE - Jim and Madge Larrabee here, which you used to know in early days, they have picked up a girl at 'Omburg, where her sister had been havin' a strong affair of the 'eart with a very 'igh young foreign nob who promised to marry 'er—but the family stepped in and threw the whole thing down. 'E be'aved very bad to 'er an had let 'imself out an written her letters an given her rings and tokens, yer see—and there was photographs too. Now as these various things showed how 'e'd deceived and betrayed 'er, they wouldn't look nice at all considerin' who the young man was, an' wot 'igh titles he was comin' into. So when this girl up an' dies of it all, these letters and things all fall into the 'ands of the sister—which is the one my friends 'ere has been nursin' all along—together with 'er mother.

BASSICK - (to LARRABEE) Where have you had the people?

LARRABEE - We took a house up the Norrington Road.

BASSICK - How long have you been there?

LARRABEE - Two years, the fourteenth of next month.

BASSICK - And those letters and—other evidences of the young man's misconduct—when will they reach their full value?

(LARRABEE is about to answer, but PRINCE jumps in quickly.)

PRINCE - It's now, don't you see. It's now—There's a marriage comin' on, an' there's been offers, an' the problem is to get the papers in our 'ands.

BASSICK - Where are they?

PRINCE - Why, the girl's got 'old of 'em, sir!

(BASSICK turns for explanation of this to LARRABEE)

LARRABEE - We had a safe for her to keep them in, supposing that when the time came we could open it, but the lock was out of order and we got Prince in to help us. He opened it last night, and the package containing the things was gone—she had taken them out herself.

BASSICK - What did you do when you discovered this?

PRINCE - Do—I 'adn't any more than got the box open, sir, an' given one look at it, when Sherlock Holmes rings the front door bell.

BASSICK - (intent) There—at your house?

LARRABEE - At my house.

BASSICK - He didn't get those letters?

LARRABEE - Well, he did get them, but he passed them back to the Faulkner girl.

BASSICK - (rises—in surprise) Passed them back, eh? What did that mean? (Goes down a little, thinking.)

LARRABEE - (slight shrug of shoulders) There's another thing that puzzles me. There was an accident below in the kitchen—a lamp fell off the table and scattered burning oil about, the butler came running up, yelling fire. We ran down there, and a few buckets of water put it out.

(MORIARTY suddenly appears at his desk. Lights on his face.)

MORIARTY - I have a suggestion to make. (All turn in surprise and look at MORIARTY.) The first thing we must do is to get rid of your butler —not discharge him—get rid of him. (To BASSICK.) Craigin for that! To-day! As soon as it's dark. Give him two others to help —Mr. Larrabee will send the man into the cellar for something – they'll be ready for him there. Doulton's van will get the body to the river. (MADGE shudders slightly.) It need not inconvenience you at all, Madam, we do these things quietly.

(BASSICK is writing orders.)

(To BASSICK.) What's the Seraph doing?

BASSICK - He's on the Reading job to-morrow night.

MORIARTY - Put him with Craigin to-day to help with that butler. But there's something else we want. Have you seen those letters, the photographs, and whatever else there may be? Have you seen them? Do you know what they're like?

MADGE - I have, sir. I've looked them through carefully several times

MORIARTY - Could you make me a counterfeit set of these things and tie them up so that they will look exactly like the package Sherlock Holmes held in his hand last night?

MADGE - I could manage the letters—but—

MORIARTY - If you manage the letters, I'll send some one who can manage the rest—from your description. Bassick—that old German artist —eh—

BASSICK - Leuftner.

MORIARTY - Precisely! Send Leuftner to Mrs. Larrabee at eleven. (Looks at watch.) Quarter past ten—that gives you three quarters of an hour to reach home. I shall want that counterfeit packet an eleven to-night —twelve hours to make it.

MADGE - It will be ready, sir.

MORIARTY - Good! Bassick—notify the Lascar that I may require the Gas Chamber at Stepney to-night.

BASSICK - The Gas Chamber?

MORIARTY - Yes. The one backing over the river—and have Craigin there a quarter before twelve with two others. Mr. Larrabee – (turning slightly to him)—I shall want you to write a letter to Mr. Sherlock Holmes which I shall dictate—and tonight I may require a little assistance from you both. (Taking in PRINCE with his glance.) Meet me here at eleven.

LARRABEE - This is all very well, sir, but you have said nothing about —the business arrangements. I'm not sure that!—

MORIARTY (turning front) You have no choice.

LARRABEE - No choice. (Looks fiercely to MORIARTY.)

(MADGE rises to quiet him. JOHN drops handkerchief. Pause.)

MORIARTY - (looking at him) No choice. (PRINCE aghast.) I do what I please. It pleases me to take hold of this case.

LARRABEE - (angry—crossing to desk) Well, what about pleasing me?

(BASSICK looks across at LARRABEE.)

MORIARTY - (perfectly quiet—looks at LARRABEE an instant) I am not so sure but I shall be able to do that as well. I will obtain the original letters from Miss Faulkner and negotiate the for much more than you could possibly obtain. In addition—you will have an opportunity to sell the counterfeit package to Holmes tonight, for a good round sum. And the money obtained from both these sources shall be divided as follows: you will take one hundred per cent, and I—nothing.

(Brief pause of astonishment.)

LARRABEE - Nothing!

MORIARTY - Nothing!

(LARRABEE moves to PRINCE.)

BASSICK - But we cannot negotiate those letters until we know who they incriminate. Mr. Larrabee has not yet informed us.

MORIARTY - Mr. Larrabee—(LARRABEE looks round to MORIARTY) —is wise in exercising caution. He values the keystone to his arch. But he will consent to let me know.

(LARRABEE goes to MADGE.)

MADGE - (going across to MORIARTY) Professor Moriarty, that information we would like to give— only to you. (Looking toward BASSICK.)

(MORIARTY motions BASSICK away. BASSICK moves a little. MORIARTY hands a card and pencil to MADGE from desk. MADGE writes a name and hands it to MORIARTY. He glances at name on card, then looks more closely. Looks up at MADGE astonished.)

MORIARTY - This is an absolute certainty.

LARRABEE - Absolute.

MORIARTY - It means that you have a fortune.

(PRINCE drinks in every word and look.)

Had I known this, you should hardly have had such terms.

LARRABEE - Oh well—we don't object to a—

MORIARTY - (interrupting) The arrangement is made, Mr. Larrabee —I bid you good morning. (Bowing with dignity and Pulling lever back.)

(LARRABEE, PRINCE and MADGE move toward door. Bolts, etc., slide back on door. BASSICK motions JOHN, who stands ready to conduct the party. BASSICK crosses to door. All bow a little and go out, followed by JOHN – business of door closing, bolts, etc. BASSICK turns at door and looks at MORIARTY.)

Bassick, place your men at nine to-night for Sherlock Holmes house in Baker Street.

BASSICK - You will go there yourself sir!

MORIARTY - I will go there myself—myself (Revolver out) I am the one to attend to this.

BASSICK - But this meeting to-night at twelve, to trap Holmes in the Gas Chamber in Swandem Lane.

MORIARTY - If I fail to kill him in Baker Street, we'll trap him to- night in Swandem Lane. Either way I have him, Bassick. I have him. I have him.

(Lights off gradually but not too slow on this act, and leave light on MORIARTY'S face last.)

(Music. Swell out forte for change.)

DARK CHANGE

SCENE 2

SHERLOCK HOLMES'S APARTMENTS IN BAKER STREET. EVENING

SCENE 2.—In SHERLOCK HOLMES' rooms in Baker Street—the large drawing-room of his apartments. An open, cheerful room, but not too much decorated. Rather plain. The walls are a plain tint, the ceiling ditto. The furniture is comfortable and goody but not elegant. Books, music, violins, tobacco pouches, pipes, tobacco, etc., are scattered in places about the room with some disorder. Various odd things are hung about. Some very choice pictures and etchings hang on the walls here and there, but the pictures do not have heavy gilt frames. All rather simple. The room gives more an impression of an artist's studio. A wide door up right side to hall (and thus by stairway to street door). Door communicating with bedroom or dining-room. A fireplace with cheerful grate fire burning, throwing a red glow into room. Through a large arch can be seen a laboratory and a table with chemicals and various knick- knacks. The lighting should be arranged so that after the dark change the first thing that becomes visible—even before the rest of the room—is the glow of the fire, the blue flame of the spirit lamp—and SHERLOCK HOLMES seated among cushions on the floor before the fire. Light gradually on, but still leaving the effect of only firelight.

Music stops, just as lights up.

SHERLOCK HOLMES is discovered on the floor before the fire. He is in a dressing-gown and slippers and has his pipe. HOLMES leans against the chesterfield. A violin is upon the chesterfield, and the bow near it, as if recently laid down. Other things Scattered about him. He sits smoking awhile in deep thought. Enter BILLY, the boy page, or buttons. He comes down to back of table.

BILLY - Mrs. 'Udson's compliments, sir, an' she wants to know if she can see you?

HOLMES - (without moving, looking into fire thoughtfully) Where is Mrs. Hudson?

BILLY - Downstairs in the back kitchen, sir.

HOLMES - My compliments and I don't think she can—from where she is.

BILLY - She'll be very sorry, sir.

HOLMES - Our regret will be mutual.

(BILLY hesitates.)

BILLY - She says it was terribly important, sir, as she wants to know what you'll have for your breakfast in the mornin'.

HOLMES - Same.

(Slight pause.)

BILLY - Same as when, sir?

HOLMES - This morning.

BILLY - You didn't 'ave nothing, sir—you wasn't 'ere.

HOLMES - Quite so—I won't be here tomorrow.

BILLY - Yes, sir. Was that all, sir?

HOLMES - Quite so.

BILLY - Thank you, sir.

(BILLY goes out. After long pause bell rings off. Enter BILLY.)

It's Doctor Watson, sir. You told me as I could always show 'im up.

HOLMES - Well! I should think so. (Rises and meets WATSON.)

BILLY - Yes, sir, thank you, sir. Dr. Watson, sir!

(Enter DR. WATSON. BILLY, grinning with pleasure as he passes in, goes out at once.)

HOLMES - (extending left hand to WATSON) Ah, Watson, dear fellow.

WATSON - (going to HOLMES and taking his hand) How are you, Holmes?

HOLMES - I'm delighted to see you, my dear fellow, perfectly delighted, upon my word—but—I'm sorry to observe that your wife has left you in this way.

WATSON - (laughing) She has gone on a little visit. (Puts hat on chair between bookcases.) But how did you know?

HOLMES - (goes to laboratory table and puts spirit lamp out, then turns up lamp on table. All lights up) How do I know? Now, Watson, how absurd for you to ask me such a question as that. How do I know anything? (Comes down a little way. Gives a very little sniff an instant, smelling something.) How do I know that you've opened a consulting room and resumed the practice of medicine without letting me hear a word about it? How do I know that you've been getting yourself very wet lately? That you have an extremely careless servant girl—and that you've moved your dressing-table to the other side of your room?

WATSON - (turning and looking at HOLMES in astonishment) Holmes, if you'd lived a few centuries ago, they'd have burned you alive. (Sits.)

HOLMES - Such a conflagration would have saved no considerable trouble and expense. (Strolls over to near fire.)

WATSON - Tell me, how did you know all that?

HOLMES - (pointing) Too simple to talk about. (Pointing at WATSON'S shoe.) Scratches and clumsy cuts—on the side of shoe there just where the fire strikes it, somebody scraped away crusted mud —and did it badly—badly. There's your wet feet and careless servant all on one foot. Face badly shaved on one side—used to be on left—light must have come from other side—couldn't well move your window—must have moved your dressing-table. (Goes to mantel and gets cocaine, etc.)

WATSON - Yes, by Jove! But my medical practice—I don't see how you –

HOLMES - (glancing up grieved) Now, Watson! How perfectly absurd of you to come marching in here, fairly reeking with the odour of iodoform, and with the black mark of nitrate of silver on the inner side of your right forefinger and ask me how I know—

WATSON - (interrupting with a laugh) Ha! ha! of course. But how the deuce did you know my wife was away and—

HOLMES - (breaking in) Where the deuce is your second Waistcoat button, and what the deuce is yesterday's boutonniere doing in to-day's lapel —and why the deuce do you wear the expression of a—

WATSON - (toying with a cigarette and laughing) Ha, ha, ha!

HOLMES - Ho! (Sneer.) Elementary! The child's play of deduction!

(HOLMES has a neat morocco case and a phial in hand, which he brings to the table and lays carefully upon it. As WATSON sees HOLMES with the open case he looks restless and apparently annoyed at what HOLMES is about to do, throwing cigarette on table. HOLMES opens the case and takes therefrom a hypodermic syringe, carefully adjusting the needle. Fills from phial. Then back left cuff of shirt a little. Pauses, looks at arm or wrist a moment. Inserts needle. Presses piston home.)

(Music. A weird bar or two—keeping on a strange pulsation on one note for cocaine business. Begin as HOLMES fills syringe.)

(WATSON has watched him with an expression of deep anxiety but with effort to restrain himself from speaking.)

WATSON - (as HOLMES puts needle in case again. Finally speaks.) Which is it to-day? Cocaine or morphine or—

HOLMES - Cocaine, my dear fellow. I'm back to my old love. A seven per cent. solution. (Offering syringe and phial.) Would you like to try some?

WATSON - (emphatically—rise) Certainly not.

HOLMES - (as if surprised) Oh! I'm sorry!

WATSON - I have no wish to break my system down before time.

(Pause.)

HOLMES - Quite right, my dear Watson—quite right—but, see, my time has come. (Goes to mantel and replaces case thereon. Throws himself languidly into chesterfield and leans back in luxurious enjoyment of the drug.)

WATSON - (goes to table, resting hand on upper corner, looking at HOLMES seriously) Holmes, for months I have seen you use these deadly drugs —in ever-increasing doses. When they lay hold of you there is no end. It must go on, and on—until the finish.

HOLMES - (lying back dreamily) So must you go on and on eating your breakfast—until the finish.

WATSON - (approaches HOLMES) Breakfast is food. These are poisons—slow but certain. They involve tissue changes of a most serious nature.

HOLMES - Just what I want. I'm bored to death with my present tissues, and I'm trying to get a brand-new lot.

WATSON - (going near HOLMES—putting hand on HOLMES' shoulder) Ah Holmes—I am trying to save you.

HOLMES - (earnest at once—places right hand on WATSON'S arm) You can't do it, old fellow—so don't waste your time.

(Music stops.)

(They look at one another an instant. WATSON sees cigarette on table —picks it up and sits.)

Watson, to change the subject a little. In the enthusiasm which has prompted you to chronicle and— if you will excuse my saying so, to somewhat embellish—a few of my little—adventures, you have occasionally committed the error—or indiscretion—of giving them a certain tinge of romance which struck me as being a trifle out of place. Something like working an elopement into the fifth proposition of Euclid. I merely refer to this in case you should see fit at some future time —to chronicle the most important and far-reaching case in my career —one upon which I have laboured for nearly fourteen months, and which is now rapidly approaching a singularly diverting climax—the case of Professor Robert Moriarty.

WATSON - Moriarty! I don't remember ever having heard of the fellow.

HOLMES - The Napoleon of crime. The Napoleon! Sitting motionless like an ugly venomous spider in the centre of his web—but that web having a thousand radiations and the spider knowing every quiver of every one of them.

WATSON - Really! This is very interesting. (Turns chair facing HOLMES.)

HOLMES - Ah—but the real interest will come when the Professor begins to realize his position— which he cannot fail to do shortly. By ten o'clock to-morrow night the time will be ripe for the arrests. Then the greatest criminal trial of the century ... the clearing up of over forty mysteries ... and the rope for every one.

WATSON - Good! What will he do when he sees that you have him?

HOLMES - Do? He will do me the honour, my dear Watson, of turning every resource of his wonderful organization of criminals to the one purpose of my destruction.

WATSON - Why, Holmes, this is a dangerous thing. (Rises.)

HOLMES - Dear Watson, it's perfectly delightful! It saves me any number of doses of those deadly drugs upon which you occasionally favour me with your medical views! My whole life is spent in a series of frantic endeavours to escape from the dreary common places of existence! For a brief period I escape! You should congratulate me!

WATSON - But you could escape them without such serious risks! Your other cases have not been so dangerous, and they were even more interesting. Now, the one you spoke of—the last time I saw you—the recovery of those damaging letters and gifts from a young girl who—

(HOLMES suddenly rises—stands motionless. WATSON looks at him surprised. Brief pause. Then WATSON sits in arm-chair.)

A most peculiar affair as I remember it. You were going to try an experiment of making her betray their hiding-place by an alarm of fire in her own house—and after that—

HOLMES - Precisely—after that.

(Pause.)

WATSON - Didn't the plan succeed?

HOLMES - Yes—as far as I've gone.

WATSON - You got Forman into the house as butler?

HOLMES (nods) Forman was in as butler.

WATSON - And upon your signal he overturned a lamp in the kitchen – (HOLMES moves up and down)—scattered the smoke balls and gave an alarm of fire?

(HOLMES nods and mutters "Yes" under his breath)

And the young lady—did she—

HOLMES - (turning and interrupting) Yes, she did, Watson. (Going down near him as if he had recovered himself) The young lady did. It all transpired precisely as planned. I took the packet of papers from its hiding- place—and as I told you I would handed it back to Miss Faulkner.

WATSON - But you never told me why you proposed to hand it back.

HOLMES - For a very simple reason my dear Watson That would have been theft for me to take it. The contents of the packet were the absolute property of the young lady.

WATSON - What did you gain by this?

HOLMES - Her confidence, and so far as I was able to secure it, her regard. As it was impossible for me to take possession of the letters, photographs and jewellery in that packet without her consent, my only alternative is to obtain that consent—to induce her to give it to me of her own free will. Its return to her after I had laid hands on it was the first move in this direction. The second will depend entirely upon what transpires to- day. I expect Forman here to report in half an hour.

(Light hurried footsteps outside. Short quick knock at door and enter TÉRÉSE in great haste and excitement. WATSON rises and turns and faces her near table. HOLMES turns towards fire-place.)

TÉRÉSE - I beg you to pardon me, sir, ze boy he say to come right up as soon as I come.

HOLMES - Quite right! quite right!

TÉRÉSE - Ah! I fear me zere is trouble—Messieurs —ze butlair—you assesstant—ze one who sent me to you –

HOLMES - Forman? (Turning to her.)

TÉRÉSE - Heem! Forman. Zere ees somesing done to heem! I fear to go down to see.

HOLMES - Down where?

(WATSON watches.)

TÉRÉSE - Ze down. (Gesture.) Ze cellaire of zat house. Eet ees a dreadful place. He deed not come back. He went down—he deed not return. (Business of anguish.)

(HOLMES goes to table—rings bell and takes revolver from drawer and slides it into his hip pocket, at same time unfastening dressing- gown.)

HOLMES - (during business) Who sent him down?

TÉRÉSE - M'sjeur of ze house, M'sieur Chetwood.

HOLMES - Larrabee?

TÉRESE -Yes.

HOLMES - (during business) Has he been down there long?

TÉRÉSE - No—for I soon suspect—ze dreadful noise was heard. Oh—(covers face)—ze noise! Ze noise!

HOLMES - What noise? (Goes to her and seizes her arm.)

TÉRÉSE - Ze noise!

HOLMES - Try to be calm and answer me. What did it sound like?

TÉRÉSE - Ze dreadful cry of a man who eez struck down by a deadly seeng.

(Enter BILLY)

HOLMES - Billy! Coat—boots, and order a cab—quick! (Back again to table, takes a second revolver out.)

BILLY - (darting off at door) Yes, sir.

HOLMES - (to TÉRÉSE) Did anyone follow him down?

(BILLY is back in a second.)

TÉRÉSE - I did not see.

HOLMES - Don't wait. The cab.

(BILLY shoots off having placed coat over chesterfield and boots on floor)

Take this Watson and come with me. (Handing WATSON a revolver. WATSON advances a step to meet HOLMES and takes revolver.)

TÉRÉSE - I had not better go also?

HOLMES - No … Wait here! (Ready to go. About to take off dressing gown)

(Hurried footsteps heard outside)

(Pause.) Ha! I hear Forman coming now.

(Enter FORMAN.)

TÉRÉSE - (seeing FORMAN—under her breath) Ah! (Backing a little)

(FORMAN coming rapidly on is covered with black coal stains, and his clothing otherwise stained. He has a bad bruise on forehead. But he must not be made to look grotesque. There must be no suspicion of comedy about his entrance. Also he must not be torn, as BILLY is later in the scene. HOLMES just above table stops taking off his dressing gown, slips it back on shoulders again.)

FORMAN - (to HOLMES in an entirely matter of fact tone) Nothing more last night, sir. After you left, Prince came in, they made a start for her room to get the package away, but I gave the three knocks with an axe on the floor beams as you directed, and they didn't go any farther. This morning, a little after nine—

HOLMES - One moment.

FORMAN - Yes, sir?

HOLMES - (quietly turns to TÉRÉSE) Mademoiselle —step into that room and rest yourself. (Indicating bedroom door.)

TÉRÉSE - (who has been deeply interested in FORMAN'S report) Ah! (Shaking head.) I am not tired, Monsieur.

HOLMES - Step in and walk about, then. I'll let you know when you are required.

TÉRÉSE - (after an instant's pause sees it) Oui, Monsieur. (Goes out.)

(HOLMES goes over and quickly closes the door after her—he then turns to WATSON, but remains at the door with right ear alert to catch any sound from within.)

HOLMES - Take a look at his head, Watson. (Listens at door.)

(WATSON at once goes to FORMAN.)

FORMAN - It's nothing at all.

HOLMES - Take a look at his head, Watson.

WATSON - An ugly bruise, but not dangerous. (Examining head.)

(WATSON goes quickly and stands near end of chesterfield facing around to FORMAN.)

HOLMES - Very well ... At a little after nine, you say – (HOLMES has attention on door, where TÉRÉSE went off while listening to FORMAN—but not in such a marked way as to take the attention off from what he says, and after a few seconds sits on chesterfield)

FORMAN - Yes, sir! (Coming down a little.) This morning a little after nine, Larrabee and his wife drove away and she returned about eleven without him. A little later, old Leuftner came and the two went to work in the library. I got a look at them from the outside and found they were making up a counterfeit of the Package we're working for! You'll have to watch for some sharp trick, sir.

HOLMES - They'll have to watch for the trick, my dear Forman. And Larrabee what of him?

FORMAN - He came back a little after three

HOLMES - How did he seem?

FORMAN - Under great excitement, sir.

HOLMES - Any marked resentment towards you?

FORMAN - I think there was, sir—though he tried not to show it.

HOLMES - He has consulted some one outside. Was the Larrabee woman's behaviour different also?

FORMAN - Now I come to think of it, she gave me an ugly look as she came in.

HOLMES - Ah, an ugly look. She was present at the consultation. They were advised to get you out of the way. He sent you into the cellar on some pretext. You were attacked in the dark by two men— possibly three —and received a bad blow from a sand club. You managed to strike down one of your assailants with a stone or piece of timber and escaped from the others in the dark crawling out through a coal grating.

FORMAN - That's what took place sir.

HOLMES - They've taken in a partner, and a dangerous one at that. He not only directed this conspiracy against you, but he advised the making of the counterfeit package as well. Within a very short time I shall receive an offer from Larrabee to sell the package of letters. He will indicate that Miss Faulkner changed her mind, and has concluded to get what she can for them. He will desire to meet me on the subject—and will then endeavour to sell me his bogus package for a large sum of money. After that—

(Enter BILLY with a letter)

BILLY - Letter, sir! Most important letter, sir! (After giving HOLMES letter, he stands waiting.)

HOLMES - Unless I am greatly mistaken—the said communication is at hand. (Lightly waves letter across before face once getting the scent.) It is. Read it, Watson, there's a good fellow, my eyes – (With a motion across eyes. Half smile.) You know, cocaine—and all those things you like so much.

(BILLY goes with letter to WATSON. WATSON takes letter and up to lamp.)

WATSON (opens letter and reads) "Dear Sir."

(After WATSON is at lamp, FORMAN waits.)

HOLMES - Who—thus—addresses me? (Slides further on to chesterfield, supporting head on pillows.)

WATSON - (glances at signature) "James Larrabee."

HOLMES - (whimsically) What a surprise! And what has James to say this evening?

WATSON - "Dear Sir."

HOLMES - I hope he won't say that again.

WATSON - "I have the honour to inform you that Miss Faulkner has changed her mind regarding the letters, etc., which you wish to obtain, and has decided to dispose of them for a monetary consideration. She has placed them in my hands for this purpose, and if you are in a position to offer a good round sum, and to pay it down at once in cash, the entire lot is yours. If you wish to negotiate, however, it must be to-night, at the house of a friend of mine, in the city. At eleven o'clock you will be at the Guards' Monument at the foot of Waterloo Place. You will see a cab with wooden shutters to the windows. Enter it and the driver will bring you to my friend's house. If you have the cab followed, or try any other underhand trick, you won't get what you want. Let me know your decision. Yours truly, James Larrabee."

(HOLMES during the reading of the letter begins to write something in a perfectly leisurely way. The light of the fire is upon him, shining across the room—on his left—as he writes.)

HOLMES - Now see if I have the points. To-night, eleven o'clock – Guards' Monument—cab with wooden shutters. No one to come with me. No one to follow cab—or I don't get what I want.

WATSON - Quite right.

HOLMES - Ah!

WATSON - But this cab with the wooden shutters. (Coming down and placing letter on table.)

HOLMES - A little device to keep me from seeing where I am driven. Billy!

BILLY - (going to HOLMES at once) Yes, sir.

HOLMES - (reaching out letter to BILLY back of him without looking) Who brought it?

BILLY - It was a woman, sir.

HOLMES - (slight dead stop as he is handing letter) Ah—old young? (He does not look round for these questions, but faces the was front or nearly so)

BILLY - Werry old sir.

HOLMES - In a cab?

BILLY - Yes, sir.

HOLMES - Seen the driver before?

BILLY - Yes sir—but I cant think where.

HOLMES - (rising) Hand this over to the old lady—apologize for the delay and look at the driver again.

BILLY - (takes letter) Yes sir. (Goes out)

WATSON - My dear Holmes—you did not say you would go?

HOLMES - Certainly I did.

WATSON - But it is the counterfeit.

HOLMES - (moves towards bedroom door) The counterfeit is what I want.

WATSON - Why so?

HOLMES - (turning to WATSON an instant) Because with it I shall obtain the original (Turns and speaks off at door.) Mademoiselle! (Turns back)

WATSON - But this fellow means mischief.

(Enter TÉRESE She comes into and stands a little way inside the room)

HOLMES (facing WATSON—touching himself lightly) This fellow means the same.

(As HOLMES turns away to TÉRÉSE, WATSON crosses and stands with back to fire)

(To TÉRÉSE) Be so good Mademoiselle as to listen to every word. To-night at twelve o'clock I meet Mr. Larrabee and purchase from him the false bundle of letters to which you just now heard us refer, as you were listening at the keyhole of the door.

TÉRÉSE - (slightly confused but staring blankly) Oui, Monsieur.

HOLMES - I wish Miss Faulkner to know at once that I propose to buy this package to night.

TÉRÉSE - I will tell her, Monsieur.

HOLMES - That is my wish. But do not tell her that I know this packet and its contents to be counterfeit. She is to suppose that I think I am buying the genuine.

TÉRÉSE - Oui, Monsieur, je comprends. When you purchase you think you have the real.

HOLMES - Precisely. (Motions her up to door and moving towards door with her.) One thing more. Tomorrow evening I shall want you to accompany her to this place, here. Sir Edward Leighton and Count von Stalburg will be here to receive the package from me. However, you will receive further instructions as to this in the morning.

TÉRÉSE - Oui, Monsieur. (Turns and goes out at once.)

HOLMES - Forman.

FORMAN - Yes, sir.

HOLMES - Change to your beggar disguise No. 14 and go through every place in the Riverside District. Don't stop till you get a clue to this new partner of the Larrabees. I must have that. (Turns away towards WATSON.) I must have that.

FORMAN - Very well, sir. (Just about to go.)

(Enter BILLY.)

BILLY - If you please, sir, there's a man a-waitin' at the street door —and 'e says 'e must speak to Mr. Forman, sir, as quick as 'e can.

(HOLMES—who was moving—stops suddenly and stands motionless—eyes front. Pause.)

(Music. Danger. Melodramatic. Very low. Agitato. B String.)

HOLMES (after a pause) We'd better have a look at that man, Billy, show him up.

BILLY - 'E can't come up, sir—'e's a-watchin' a man in the Street. 'E says 'e's from Scotland Yard.

FORMAN (going toward door) I'd better see what it is, sir.

HOLMES - No!

(FORMAN stops. Pause. Music heard throughout this pause, but without swelling forte in the least. HOLMES stands motionless a moment)

Well—(a motion indicating FORMAN to go)—take a look at first. Be ready for anything.

FORMAN - Trust me for that, sir. (Goes out.)

HOLMES - Billy, see what he does.

BILLY - Yes, sir.

(HOLMES stands an instant thinking)

WATSON - This is becoming interesting.

(HOLMES does not reply He goes up to near door and listens then moves to window and glances down to street then turns goes down to table)

Look here Holmes you've been so kind as to give me a half look into this case—

HOLMES - (looking up at him) What case?

WATSON - This strange case of—Miss—

HOLMES - Quite so. One moment my dear fellow (Rings bell.)

(After slight wait enter BILLY)

Mr. Forman—is he there still?

BILLY - No, sir—'e's gone. (Second's pause.)

HOLMES - That's all.

BILLY - Yes sir. Thank you sir. (Goes out)

(Music stops)

HOLMES - As you were saying, Watson. (Eyes front.) strange case —of—(Stops but does not change position. As if listening or thinking)

WATSON - Of Miss Faulkner.

HOLMES - (abandoning further anxiety and giving attention to WATSON) Precisely. This strange case of Miss Faulkner. (Eyes down an instant as he recalls it)

WATSON - You've given me some idea of it. Now don't you it would be only fair to let me have the rest?

(HOLMES looks at him)

HOLMES - What shall I tell you?

WATSON - Tell me what you propose to do with that counterfeit package —which you are going to risk your life to obtain.

(HOLMES looks at WATSON an instant before speaking.)

HOLMES - I intend, with the aid of the counterfeit, to make her willingly hand me the genuine. I shall accomplish this by a piece of trickery and deceit of which I am heartily ashamed—and which I would never have undertaken if I—if I had known her—as I do now (Looks to the front absently.) It's too bad. She's—she's rather a nice girl, Watson. (Goes over to mantel and gets a pipe.)

WATSON - (following HOLMES with his eyes) Nice girl, is she?

(HOLMES nods "Yes" to WATSON. Brief pause. He turns with pipe in hands and glances towards WATSON, then down.)

Then you think that possibly—

(Enter BILLY quickly.)

BILLY - I beg pardon, sir, Mr. Forman's just sent over from the chemist's on the corner to say 'is 'ead is a-painin' 'im a bit, an' would Dr. Watson –

(WATSON, on hearing his name, turns and looks in direction of BILLY)

—kindly step over and get 'im something to put on it.

WATSON - (moving at once towards door) Yes—certainly – I'll go at once. (Picking up hat off chair.) That's singular. (Stands puzzled.) It didn't look like anything serious. (At door.) I'll be back in a minute, Holmes. (Goes out.)

(HOLMES says nothing.)

HOLMES - Billy.

BILLY - Yes, sir.

HOLMES - Who brought that message from Forman?

BILLY - Boy from the chemist's, sir.

HOLMES - Yes, of course, but which boy?

BILLY - Must-a-bin a new one, sir—I ain't never seen 'im before.

(Music. Danger. Melodramatic. Very low. Agitato.)

HOLMES - Quick, Billy, run down and look after the doctor. If the boy's gone and there's a man with him it means mischief. Let me know, quick. Don't stop to come up, ring the door bell. I'll hear it. Ring it loud. Quick now.

BILLY - Yes, sir. (Goes out quickly.)

(HOLMES waits motionless a moment, listening.)

(Music heard very faintly.)

(HOLMES moves quickly towards door. When half-way to the door he stops suddenly, listening; then begins to glide backward toward table, stops and listens—eyes to the front; turns towards door listening. Pipe in left hand—waits—sees pipe in hand—picks up match – lights pipe, listening, and suddenly shouts of warning from BILLY – turns—at the same time picking up revolver from off table and puts in pocket of dressing-gown, with his hand clasping it. HOLMES at once assumes easy attitude, but keeps eyes on door. Enter MORIARTY. He walks in at door very quietly and deliberately. Stops just within doorway, and looks fixedly at HOLMES, then moves forward a little way. His right hand behind his back. As MORIARTY moves forward, HOLMES makes slight motion for the purpose of keeping him covered with revolver in his pocket. MORIARTY, seeing what HOLMES is doing, stops.)

MORIARTY - (very quiet low voice) It is a dangerous habit to finger loaded firearms in the pocket of one's dressing-gown.

HOLMES - You'll be taken from here to the hospital if you keep that hand behind you.

(After slight pause MORIARTY slowly takes his hand from behind his back and holds it with the other in front of him.)

In that case, the table will do quite as well. (Places his revolver on the table.)

MORIARTY - You evidently don't know me.

HOLMES - (takes pipe out of mouth, holding it. With very slight motion toward revolver) I think it quite evident that I do. Please take a chair, Professor. (Indicating arm-chair.) I can spare five minutes —if you have anything to say.

(Very slight pause—then MORIARTY moves his right hand as if to take something from inside his coat. Stops instantly on HOLMES covering him with revolver, keeping hand exactly where it was stopping.)

What were you about to do?

MORIARTY - Look at my watch.

HOLMES - I'll tell you when the five minutes is up.

(Slight pause. MORIARTY comes slowly forward. He advances to back of arm- chair. Stands motionless there an instant, his eyes on HOLMES. He then takes off his hat, and stoops slowly, putting it on floor, eyeing HOLMES the while. He then moves down a little to right of chair, by its side. HOLMES now places revolver on table, but before he has quite let go of it, MORIARTY raises his right hand, whereupon HOLMES quietly takes the revolver back and holds it at his side. MORIARTY has stopped with right hand near his throat, seeing HOLMES' business with revolver. He now slowly pulls away a woolen muffler from his throat and stands again with hands down before him. HOLMES' forefinger motionless on table. MORIARTY moves a little in front of chair. This movement is only a step or two. As he makes it HOLMES moves simultaneously on the other side of the table so that he keeps the revolver between them on the table. That is the object of this business.)

MORIARTY - All that I have to say has already crossed your mind.

HOLMES - My answer thereto has already crossed yours.

MORIARTY - It is your intention to pursue this case against me?

HOLMES - That is my intention to the very end.

MORIARTY - I regret this—not so much on my own account—but on yours.

HOLMES - I share your regrets, Professor, but solely because of the rather uncomfortable position it will cause you to occupy.

MORIARTY - May I inquire to what position you are pleased to allude, Mr. Holmes?

(HOLMES motions a man being hanged with his left hand—slight Pause. A tremor of passion. MORIARTY slowly advances towards HOLMES. He stops instantly as HOLMES' hand goes to his revolver, having only approached him a step or two.)

And have you the faintest idea that you would be permitted to live to see the day?

HOLMES - As to that, I do not particularly care, so that I might bring you to see it.

(MORIARTY makes a sudden impulsive start towards HOLMES, but stops on being covered with revolver. He has now come close to the table on the other side of HOLMES. This tableau is held briefly.)

MORIARTY - (passionately but in a low tone) You will never bring me to see it. You will find—(He stops, recollecting himself as HOLMES looks at him—changes to quieter tone.) Ah! you are a bold man Mr. Holmes to insinuate such a thing to my face—(turning towards front)—but it is the boldness born of ignorance. (Turning still further away from HOLMES in order to get his back to him and after doing so suddenly raising his right hand to breast he is again stopped with hand close to pocket by hearing the noise of HOLMES'S revolver behind him. He holds that position for a moment then passes the matter off by feeling muffler as if adjusting it. He mutters to himself) You'll never bring me to see it, you'll never bring me to see it (Then begins to move in front of table still keeping his back towards HOLMES. Business as he moves forward of stopping suddenly on hearing the noise of revolver sliding along table then when in front of table slowly turns so that he brings his hands into view of HOLMES then a slight salute with hand and bow and back slowly with dignity into chair)

(Business of HOLMES seating himself on stool opposite MORIARTY, revolver business and coming motionless)

(After HOLMES'S business.) I tell you it is the boldness born of ignorance. Do you think that I would be here if I had not made the streets quite safe in every respect?

HOLMES - (shaking head) Oh no! I could never so grossly overestimate your courage as that.

MORIARTY - Do you imagine that your friend the doctor, and your man Forman will soon return?

HOLMES - Possibly not.

MORIARTY - So it leaves us quite alone—doesn't it, Mr. Holmes —quite alone—so that we can talk the matter over quietly and not be disturbed. In the first place I wish to call your attention to a few memoranda which I have jotted down—(suddenly put both hands to breast pocket)—which you will find—

HOLMES - Look out! Take your hands away.

(Music: Danger pp)

(MORIARTY again stopped with his hands at breast pocket)

Get your hands down.

(MORIARTY does not lower his hands at first request.)

A little further away from the memorandum book you are talking about.

MORIARTY - (lowers hands to his lap. Slight pause, raising hands again slowly as he speaks) Why, I was merely about to—

HOLMES - Well, merely don't do it.

MORIARTY - (remonstratingly—his hands still up near breast) But I would like to show you a—

HOLMES - I don't want to see it.

MORIARTY - But if you will allow me—

HOLMES - I don't care for it at all. I don't require any notebooks. If you want it so badly we'll have someone get it for you.

(MORIARTY slowly lowers hands again.)

(Rings bell on table with left hand.) I always like to save my guests unnecessary trouble.

MORIARTY - (after quite a pause) I observe that your boy does not answer the bell.

HOLMES - No. But I have an idea that he will before long.

MORIARTY - (leaning towards HOLMES and speaking with subdued rage and significance) It may possibly be longer than you think, Mr. Holmes.

HOLMES - (intensely) What! That boy!

MORIARTY - (hissing at HOLMES) Yes, your boy.

(Hold the tableau for a moment, the two men scowling at each other. HOLMES slowly reaching left hand out to ring bell again. MORIARTY begins to raise right hand slowly towards breast pocket, keeping it concealed beneath his muffler as far as possible. On slight motion of HOLMES' left hand, he lowers it again, giving up the attempt this time.)

HOLMES - At least we will try the bell once more, Professor. (Rings bell.)

(Short wait.)

MORIARTY - (after pause) Doesn't it occur to you that he may Possibly have been detained, Mr. Holmes?

HOLMES - It does. But I also observe that you are in very much the same predicament. (Pause.)

(HOLMES rings bell for the third time. Noise on stairway outside. Enter BILLY with part of his coat, and with sleeves of shirt and waistcoat badly torn)

(Music stops)

BILLY - (up near door) I beg pardon, sir—someone tried to 'old me sir! (Panting for breath)

HOLMES - It is quite evident however that he failed to do so.

BILLY - Yes sir—'e's got my coat sir but 'e 'asn't got me!

HOLMES - Billy!

BILLY - (cheerfully) Yes sir (Still out of breath)

HOLMES - The gentleman I am pointing out to you with this six-shooter desires to have us get something out of his left hand coat pocket.

(MORIARTY gives a very slight start or movement of right hand to breast pocket, getting it almost to his pocket, then recollecting himself, seeing that HOLMES has got him covered)

Ah, I thought so. Left-hand coat pocket. As he is not feeling quite himself to-day, and the exertion might prove injurious, suppose you attend to it.

BILLY - Yes sir (He goes quickly to MORIARTY puts hand in his pocket and draws out a bull dog revolver) Is this it sir?

HOLMES - It has the general outline of being it. Quite so. Put it on the table.

(MORIARTY makes a grab for it)

Not there Billy. Look out. Push it a little further this way.

(BILLY does so placing it so that it is within easy reach of HOLMES.)

HOLMES - That's more like it.

BILLY - Shall I see if he's got another sir?

HOLMES - Why, Billy, you surprise me, after the gentleman has taken the trouble to inform you that he hasn't.

BILLY - When sir?

HOLMES - When he made a snatch for this one. Now that we have your little memorandum book, Professor, do you think of anything else you'd like before Billy goes?

(MORIARTY does not reply.)

Any little thing that you've got, that you want? No! Ah, I am sorry that's all, Billy.

(pause. MORIARTY motionless, eyes on HOLMES. HOLMES puts his own revolver in his pocket quietly. MORIARTY remains motionless, his eyes on HOLMES, waiting for a chance.)

BILLY - Thank you, sir. (Goes out.)

(HOLMES carelessly picks up MORIARTY'S weapon, turns it over in his hands a little below table for a moment, then tosses it back on table again —during which business MORIARTY looks front savagely.)

HOLMES - (tapping revolver with pipe) Rather a rash project of yours Moriarty—even though you have made the street quite safe in every respect—to make use of that thing—so early in the evening and in this part of the town.

MORIARTY - Listen to me. On the 4th of January you crossed my path – on the 23rd you incommoded me. And now, at the close of April, I find myself placed in such a position through your continual interference that I am in positive danger of losing my liberty.

HOLMES - Have you any suggestion to make?

MORIARTY - (head swaying from side to side) No! (Pause and look fiercely at HOLMES.) I have no suggestion to make. I have a fact to state. If you do not drop it at once your life is not worth that. (Snap of finger.)

HOLMES - I shall be pleased to drop it—at ten o'clock to- morrow night.

MORIARTY - Why then?

HOLMES - Because at that hour, Moriarty ... your life will not be worth that, (A snap of finger.) You will be under arrest.

MORIARTY - At that hour, Sherlock Holmes, your eyes will be closed in death.

(Both look at one another motionless an instant.)

HOLMES - (rising as if rather bored) I am afraid, Professor, that in the pleasure of this conversation I am neglecting more important business. (Turns away to mantel and business of looking for match, etc.)

(MORIARTY rises slowly, picks up hat, keeping his eyes on HOLMES. Suddenly catches sight of revolver on table—pause—and putting hat on table.)

MORIARTY - (nearing HOLMES and looking towards door) I came here this evening to see if peace could not be arranged between us.

HOLMES - Ah yes (Smiling pleasantly and pressing tobacco in pipe.) I saw that. That's rather good.

MORIARTY - (passionately) You have seen fit not only to reject my proposals, but to make insulting references coupled with threats of arrest.

HOLMES - Quite so! Quite so! (Lights match and holds it to pipe)

MORIARTY - (moving a little so as to be nearer table) Well (slyly picking up revolver)—you have been warned of your danger – you do not heed that warning—perhaps you will heed this!

(Making a sudden plunge and aiming at HOLMES' head rapidly snaps the revolver in quick attempt to fire)

(HOLMES turns quietly toward him still holding match to pipe so that the last snap of hammer is directly in his face. Very slight pause on MORIARTY being unable to fire—and back up at same time boiling with rage.)

HOLMES - Oh! ha!—here! (As if recollecting something. Tosses away match and feeling quickly in left pocket of dressing gown brings out some cartridges and tosses them carelessly on table towards MORIARTY.) I didn't suppose you'd want to use that thing again, so I took all your cartridges out and put them in my pocket. You'll find them all there, Professor. (Reaches over and rings bell on table with right hand.)

(Enter BILLY)

Billy!

BILLY - Yes, sir!

HOLMES - Show this gentleman nicely to the door.

BILLY - Yes sir! This way sir! (Standing within door)

(PROFESSOR MORIARTY looks at HOLMES a moment, then flings revolver down and across the table, clenches fist in HOLMES' face, turns boiling with rage, picks hat up, and exits quickly at door, muttering aloud as he goes.)

HOLMES - (after exit of MORIARTY) Billy! Come here!

BILLY - Yes, sir! (BILLY comes quickly down.)

HOLMES - Billy! You're a good boy!

BILLY - Yes, sir! Thank you, sir! (Stands grinning up at HOLMES.)

(The lights go out suddenly.)

(No music at end of this Act.)

CURTAIN

ACT III

THE STEPNEY GAS CHAMBER. MIDNIGHT

SCENE.—The Gas Chamber at Stepney. A large, dark, grimy room on an upper floor of an old building backing on wharves etc. Plaster cracking off, masonry piers or chimney showing. As uncanny and gruesome appearance as possible. Heavy beams and timbers showing. Door leads to the landing and then to the entrance. Another door leads to a small cupboard. The walls of the cupboard can be seen when the door is opened. Large window, closed. Grimy and dirty glass so nothing can be seen through it. The window is nailed with spike nails securely shut. Black backing—no light behind. Strong bars outside back of windows, to show when window is broken. These bars must not be seen through the glass. Trash all over the room. The only light in the room on the rise of the curtain is from a dim lantern—carried on by McTAGUE.

Characteristic Music for Curtain.

CRAIGIN and LEARY are discovered. CRAIGIN is sitting on a box. He sits glum and motionless, waiting. LEARY is sitting on table his feet on the chair in front of it.

McTAGUE enters with safety lamp. He stops just within a moment, glancing around in the dimness. Soon moves up near a masonry pier, a little above the door, and leans against it, waiting. CRAIGIN, LEARY and McTAGUE are dressed in dark clothes and wear felt-soled shoes.

LEARY - What's McTague doing 'ere?

McTAGUE - I was sent 'ere.

(All dialogue in this part of Act in low tones, but distinct, to give a weird effect, echoing through the large grimy room among the deep shadows.)

LEARY - I thought the Seraph was with us in this job.

CRAIGIN - 'E ain't.

LEARY - Who was the last you put the gas on?

(Pause.)

CRAIGIN - I didn't 'ear 'is name. (Pause.) 'E'd been 'oldin' back money on a 'aul out some railway place.

(Pause.)

McTAGUE - What's this 'ere job he wants done? (Sits on box, placing lamp on floor by his side.)

(Pause.)

CRAIGIN - I ain't been told.

(Pause.)

LEARY - As long as it's 'ere we know what it's likely to be.

(Door opens slowly and hesitatingly. Enter SID PRINCE. He stands just within door, and looks about a little suspiciously as if uncertain what to do. Pause. He notices that the door is slowly closing behind him and quietly holds it back. But he must not burlesque this movement with funny business. McTAGUE holds lantern up to see who it is, at the same time rising and coming down near PRINCE.)

PRINCE - Does any one of you blokes know if this is the place where I meet Alf Bassick?

(Pause. Neither of the other men take notice of PRINCE. McTAGUE goes back to where he was sitting before PRINCE'S entrance.)

(After waiting a moment.) From wot you say, I take it you don't.

CRAIGIN - We ain't knowin' no such man. 'E may be 'ere and 'e may not.

PRINCE - Oh! (Comes a little farther into room and lets the door close.) It's quite right then, thank you. (Pause. No one speaks.) Nice old place to find, this 'ere is. (No one answers him.) And when you do find it—(looks about)—I can't say it's any too cheerful. (He thereupon pulls out a cigarette- case, puts a cigarette in his mouth, and feels in pocket for matches. Finds one. About to light it. Has moved a few steps during this.)

CRAIGIN - Here! ...

(PRINCE stops.)

Don't light that! ... It ain't safe!

(PRINCE stops motionless, where above speech caught him, for an instant. Pause. PRINCE begins to turn his head slowly and only a little way, glances carefully about, as if expecting to see tins of nitro-glycerine. He sees nothing on either side, and finally turns towards CRAIGIN.)

PRINCE - If it ain't askin' too much wot's the matter with the place? It looks all roight to me.

CRAIGIN - Well don't light no matches, and it'll stay lookin' the same.

(Pause. Door opens, and BASSICK enters hurriedly. He looks quickly about.)

BASSICK - Oh, Prince, you're here. I was looking for you outside.

PRINCE - You told me to be 'ere, sir. That was 'ow the last arrangement stood.

BASSICK - Very well! (Going across PRINCE and glancing about to see that the other men are present.) You've got the rope Craigin?

(Voices are still kept low.)

CRAIGIN (pointing to bunch of loose rope on floor near him) It's 'ere.

BASSICK - That you, Leary?

LEARY - 'Ere, sir!

BASSICK - And McTague?

McTAGUE - 'Ere, sir!

BASSICK - You want to be very careful with it to-night—you've got a tough one.

CRAIGIN - You ain't said who, as I've 'eard.

BASSICK - (low voice) Sherlock Holmes.

(Brief pause.)

CRAIGIN - (after the pause) You mean that, sir?

BASSICK - Indeed, I do!

CRAIGIN - We're goin' to count 'im out.

BASSICK - Well, if you don't and he gets away—I'm sorry for you, that's all.

CRAIGIN - I'll be cursed glad to put the gas on 'im—I tell you that.

LEARY - I say the same myself.

(Sound of MORIARTY and LARRABEE coming.)

BASSICK - Sh! Professor Moriarty's coming.

(McTAGUE places lamp on box.)

LEARY - Not the guv'nor?

BASSICK - Yes. He wanted to see this.

(The three men retire a little up stage, waiting. BASSICK moves to meet MORIARTY. PRINCE moves up out of way. Door opens. Enter MORIARTY, followed by LARRABEE. Door slowly closes behind them. LARRABEE waits a moment near door and then retires up near PRINCE. They watch the following scene. All speeches low—quiet—in undertone.)

MORIARTY - Where's Craigin?

(CRAIGIN steps forward.)

Have you got your men?

CRAIGIN - All 'ere, sir.

MORIARTY - No mistakes to-night.

CRAIGIN - I'll be careful o' that.

MORIARTY - (quick glance about) That door, Bassick. (Points up, back to audience.)

BASSICK - A small cupboard, sir. (Goes quickly up and opens the door wide to show it.)

(LEARY catches up lantern and swings it near the cupboard door.)

MORIARTY - No outlet?

BASSICK - None whatever, sir.

(LEARY swings lantern almost inside cupboard to let MORIARTY See. All this dialogue in very low tones, but distinct and Impressive. BASSICK closes door after lantern business.)

MORIARTY - (turns and points) That window?

BASSICK - (moving over a little) Nailed down, sir!

(LEARY turns and swings the lantern near window so that MORIARTY can see.)

MORIARTY - A man might break the glass.

BASSICK - If he did that he'd come against heavy iron bars outside.

CRAIGIN - We'll 'ave 'im tied down afore 'e could break any glass sir.

MORIARTY - (who has turned to CRAIGIN) Ah! You've used it before. Of course you know if it's airtight?

BASSICK - Every crevice is caulked sir.

MORIARTY - (turns and points as if at something directly over footlights) And that door?

(LEARY comes down and gives lantern a quick swing as if lighting place indicated)

BASSICK - (from same position) The opening is planked up solid sir as you can see and double thickness.

MORIARTY - Ah! (Satisfaction. Glances at door through which he entered) When the men turn the gas on him they leave by that door?

BASSICK - Yes sir.

MORIARTY - It can be made quite secure?

BASSICK - Heavy bolts on the outside sir and solid bars over all.

MORIARTY - Let me see how quick you can operate them.

BASSICK - They tie the man down, sir—there's no need to hurry.

MORIARTY - (same voice) Let me see how quick you can operate them.

BASSICK (quick order) Leary! (Motions him to door)

LEARY - (handing lamp to CRAIGIN) Yes sir! (He jumps to and goes out closing it at once and immediately the sound of sliding bolts and the dropping of bars are heard from outside)

(This is a very important effect as it is repeated at the end of the Act. CRAIGIN places lamp on box)

MORIARTY - That s all.

(Sounds of bolts withdrawn and LEARY enters and waits)

(Goes to CRAIGIN.) Craigin—you'll take your men outside that door and wait till Mr. Larrabee has had a little business interview with the gentleman. Take them up the passage to the left so Holmes does not see them as he comes in. (To BASSICK.) Who's driving the cab to night?

BASSICK - I sent O'Hagan. His orders are to drive him about for an hour so he doesn't know the distance or the direction he's going, and then stop at the small door at upper Swandem Lane. He's going to get him out there and show him to this door.

MORIARTY - The cab windows were covered, of course?

BASSICK - Wooden shutters, sir, bolted and secure. There isn't a place he can see through the size of a pin.

MORIARTY - (satisfied) Ah! ... (Looks about.) We must have a lamp here.

BASSICK - Better not, sir—there might be some gas left.

MORIARTY - You've got a light there. (Pointing to miner's safety lamp on box.)

BASSICK - It's a safety lamp, sir.

MORIARTY - A safety lamp! You mustn't have that here! The moment he sees that he'll know what you're doing and make trouble. (Sniffs.) There's hardly any gas. Go and tell Lascar we must have a good lamp.

(BASSICK goes out.)

(Looks about.) Bring that table over here.

(CRAIGIN and McTAGUE bring table.)

Now, Craigin—and the rest of you—One thing remember. No shooting to-night! Not a single shot. It can be heard in the alley below. The first thing is to get his revolver away before he has a chance to use it. Two of you attract his attention in front—the other come up on him from behind and snatch it out of his pocket. Then you have him. Arrange that, Craigin.

CRAIGIN - I'll attend to it, sir.

(The three men retire. Enter BASSICK with large lamp. Glass shade to lamp of whitish colour. BASSICK crosses to table and Places lamp on it.)

BASSICK - (to McTAGUE) Put out that lamp.

(McTAGUE is about to pick up lamp.)

CRAIGIN - Stop!

(McTAGUE waits.)

We'll want it when the other's taken away.

BASSICK - He mustn't see it, understand.

MORIARTY - Don't put it out—cover it with something.

CRAIGIN - Here! (He goes up, takes lantern, and pulling out a large box from several others places lantern within and pushes the open side against the wall so that no light from lantern can be seen from front.)

MORIARTY - That will do.

BASSICK - (approaching MORIARTY) You mustn't stay longer, sir. O'Hagan might be a little early.

MORIARTY - Mr. Larrabee—(Moving a step forward.) You understand!—they wait for you.

LARRABEE - (low—quiet) I understand, sir.

MORIARTY - I give you this opportunity to get what you can for your trouble. But anything that is found on him after you have finished—is subject—(glances at CRAIGIN and others)—to the usual division.

LARRABEE - That's all I want.

MORIARTY - When you have quite finished and got your money suppose you blow that little whistle which I observe hanging from your watch chain—and these gentlemen will take their turn.

(BASSICK holds door open for MORIARTY. LARRABEE moves up out of way as MORIARTY crosses.)

(Crosses to door. At door, turning to CRAIGIN.) And, Craigin —

(CRAIGIN crosses to MORIARTY.)

At the proper moment present my compliments to Mr. Sherlock Holmes, and say that I wish him a pleasant journey to the other side. (Goes out, followed by BASSICK.)

(LARRABEE glances about critically. As MORIARTY goes, PRINCE throws cigarette on floor in disgust, which LEARY picks up as he goes later, putting it in his pocket.)

LARRABEE - You'd better put that rope out of sight.

(CRAIGIN picks up rope, which he carries with him until he goes out later. LEARY and McTAGUE move across noiselessly at back. CRAIGIN stops an instant up stage to examine the window, looking at the caulking, etc., and shaking the frames to see that they are securely spiked. Others wait near door. He finishes at window. LARRABEE is examining package near lamp, which he has taken from his pocket. As LEARY crosses he picks up rope which was lying up centre and hides it in barrel. McTAGUE in crossing bumps up against PRINCE, and both look momentarily at each other very much annoyed.)

CRAIGIN - (joins LEARY and McTAGUE at door. Speaks to LARRABEE from door) You understand, sir, we're on this floor just around the far turn of the passage—so 'e won't see us as 'e's commin' up.

LARRABEE - I understand. (Turning to CRAIGIN.)

CRAIGIN - An' it's w'en we 'ears that whistle, eh?

LARRABEE - When you hear this whistle.

(CRAIGIN, LEARY and McTAGUE go out noiselessly. Pause. Door remains open. PRINCE, who has been very quiet during foregoing scene, begins to move a little nervously and looks about. He looks at his watch and then glances about again. LARRABEE is still near lamp, looking at package of papers which he took from his pocket.)

PRINCE - (coming down in a grumpy manner, head down, not looking at LARRABEE) Look 'ere, Jim, this sort of thing ain't so much in my line.

LARRABEE - (at table) I suppose not.

PRINCE - (still eyes about without looking at LARRABEE) When it comes to a shy at a safe or drillin' into bank vaults, I feels perfectly at 'ome, but I don't care so much to see a man—(Stops – hesitates.) Well, it ain't my line!

LARRABEE - (turning) Here! (Going to him and urging him toward door and putting package away.) All I want of you is to go down on the corner below and let me know when he comes.

PRINCE - (stops and turns to LARRABEE) 'Ow will I let you know?

LARRABEE - Have you got a whistle?

PRINCE - (pulls one out of pocket) Cert'nly.

LARRABEE - Well when you see O'Hagan driving with him Come down the alley there and blow it twice. (Urging PRINCE a little nearer door.)

PRINCE - Yes—but ain't it quite loikely to call a cab at the same time?

LARRABEE - What more do you want—take the cab and go home.

PRINCE - Oh, then you won't need me 'ere again.

LARRABEE - No.

(PRINCE turns to go.)

PRINCE - (going to door—very much relieved) Oh, very well —then I'll tear myself away. (Goes out.)

(Music. Pathetic, melodramatic, agitato, pp.)

(LARRABEE crosses to table and looks at lamp, gets two chairs and places them on either side of table; As he places second chair he stops dead as if having heard a noise outside, listens, and is satisfied all is well. Then thinking of the best way to conduct negotiations with Holmes, takes out cigar, and holds it a moment unlighted as he thinks. Then takes out match and is about to light it when ALICE FAULKNER enters. He starts up and looks at her. She stands looking at him, frightened and excited.)

(Music stops.)

LARRABEE - What do you want?

ALICE - It's true, then?

LARRABEE - How did you get to this place?

ALICE - I followed you—in a cab.

LARRABEE - What have you been doing since I came up here? Informing the police, perhaps.

ALICE - No—I was afraid he'd come—so I waited.

LARRABEE - Oh—to warn him very likely?

ALICE - Yes. (Pause.) To warn him. (Looks about room.)

LARRABEE - Then it's just as well you came up.

ALICE - I came to make sure—(Glances about.)

LARRABEE - Of what?

ALICE - That something else—is not going to be done besides – what they told me.

LARRABEE - Ah—somebody told you that something else was going to be done?

ALICE - Yes.

LARRABEE - So! We've got another spy in the house.

ALICE - You're going to swindle and deceive him—I know that. Is there anything more? (Advancing to him a little.)

LARRABEE - What could you do if there was?

ALICE - I could buy you off. Such men as you are always open to sale.

LARABEE - How much would you give?

ALICE - The genuine package—the real ones. All the proofs – everything

LARRABEE - (advancing above table, quietly but with quick interest) Have you got it with you?

ALICE - No, but I can get it.

LARRABEE - Oh—(Going to table. Slightly disappointed.) So you'll do all that for this man? You think he's your friend, I suppose?

ALICE - I haven't thought of it.

LARRABEE - Look what he's doing now. Coming here to buy those things off me.

ALICE - They're false. They're counterfeit.

LARRABEE - He thinks they're genuine, doesn't he? He'd hardly come here to buy them if he didn't.

ALICE - He may ask my permission still.

LARRABEE - Ha! (Sneer—turning away.) He won't get the chance.

ALICE (suspicious again) Won't get the chance. Then there is something else.

LARRABEE - Something else! (Turning to her.) Why, you see me here myself, don't you? I'm going to talk to him on a little business. How could I do him any harm?

ALICE - (advancing) Where are those men who came up here?

LARRABEE - What men?

ALICE - Three villainous looking men—I saw them go in at the street door—

LARRABEE - Oh—those men. They went up the other stairway. (Pointing over shoulder.) You can see them in the next building —if you look out of this window. (Indicating window.)

(ALICE at once goes rapidly toward the window and making a hesitating pause near table as she sees LARRABEE crossing above her but moving on again quickly LARRABEE at same time crosses well up stage, keeping his eye on ALICE as she moves towards the window and tries to look out, but finding she cannot she turns at once to LARRABEE. He is standing near door.)

(Music. Melodramatic. Danger. Keep down. pp Agitato)

(Hold this an instant where they stand looking at one another, ALICE beginning to see she has been trapped.)

ALICE - (starting toward door) I'll look in the passage-way, if you please.

LARRABEE - (taking one step down before door, quietly) Yes – but I don't please.

ALICE - (stops before him) You wouldn't dare to keep me here.

LARRABEE - I might dare—but I won't. You'd be in the way.

ALICE - Where are those men?

LARRABEE - Stay where you are and you'll see them very soon.

(LARRABEE goes to door and blows whistle as quietly as possible. Short pause. No footsteps heard, as the men move noiselessly. Enter CRAIGIN, McTAGUE and LEARY, appearing suddenly noiselessly. They stand looking in some astonishment at ALICE.)

(Music stops.)

ALICE - I knew it. (Moving back a step, seeing from this that they are going to attack Holmes.) Ah! (Under breath. After pause she turns and hurries to window, trying to look out or give an alarm. Then runs to cupboard door. LARRABEE watching her movements. Desperately.) You're going to do him some harm.

LARRABEE - Oh no, it's only a little joke—at his expense.

ALICE - (moving toward him a little) You wanted the letters, the package I had in the safe! I'll get it for you. Let me go and I'll bring it here—or whatever you tell me—(LARRABEE sneers meaningly.) I'll give you my word not to say anything to anyone – not to him—not to the policemen—not anyone!

LARRABEE - (without moving) You needn't take the trouble to get it —but you can tell me where it is—and you'll have to be quick about it too—

ALICE - Yes—if you'll promise not to go on with this.

LARRABEE - Of course! That's understood.

ALICE - (excitedly) You promise!

LARRABEE - Certainly I promise. Now where is it?

ALICE - Just outside my bedroom window—just outside on the left, fastened between the shutter and the wall—you can easily find it.

LARRABEE - Yes—I can easily find it.

ALICE - Now tell them—tell them to go.

LARRABEE - (going down to men) Tie her up so she can't make a noise. Keep her out there until we have Holmes in here, and then let O'Hagan keep her in his cab. She mustn't get back to the house— not till I've been there.

(ALICE listens dazed, astonished.)

CRAIGIN - (speaks low) Go an' get a hold, Leary. Hand me a piece of that rope.

(McTAGUE brings rope from under his coat. Business of getting rapidly ready to gag and tie ALICE. Much time must not be spent on this; quick, business-like. McTAGUE takes handkerchief from pocket to use as gag.)

LARRABEE (taking a step or two down before ALICE so as to attract her attention front) Now then, my pretty bird—(ALICE begins to move back in alarm and looking at LARRABEE.)

ALICE - You said—you said if I told you—

LARRABEE - Well—we haven't done him any harm yet, have we?

(LEARY is moving quietly round behind her.)

ALICE - Then send them away.

LARRABEE - Certainly. Go away now, boys, there's no more work for you to- night.

ALICE - (looking at them terrified) They don't obey you. They are –

(LEARY seizes her. She screams and resists, but CRAIGIN and McTAGUE come at once, so that she is quickly subdued and gagged with handkerchief, etc., and her hands tied. As the Struggle takes place, men work up to near cupboard with ALICE. LARRABEE also eagerly watching them tie ALICE up. This is not prolonged more than is absolutely necessary. Just as they finish, a shrill whistle is heard in distance outside at back, as if from street far below. All stop—listening—picture.)

CRAIGIN - Now out of the door with her—(Starting to door)

(The prolonged shrill whistle is heard again)

LARRABEE - By God, he's here.

CRAIGIN - What!

LARRABEE - That's Sid Prince, I put him on the watch.

CRAIGIN - We won't have time to get her out.

LARRABEE - Shut her in there (Pointing to cupboard)

LEARY - Yes—that'll do.

CRAIGIN - In with her.

(LEARY and CRAIGIN, almost on the word, take her to cup board. McTAGUE goes and keeps watch at door.)

(As he holds ALICE.) Open that door! Open that door!

(LEARY goes and opens cupboard door. As LEARY leaves she breaks away from CRAIGIN and gets almost to right when CRAIGIN catches her again. As he takes hold of her she faints, and he throws her into cupboard in a helpless condition. LEARY closes cupboard door and they stand before it.)

LEARY - (still at cupboard door. Others have turned so as to avoid suspicion if Holmes comes in on them) There ain't no lock on this 'ere door.

LARRABEE - No lock!

LEARY - No.

LARRABEE - Drive something in.

CRAIGIN - Here, this knife. (Hands LEARY a large clasp-knife, opened ready.)

LARRABEE - A knife won't hold it.

CRAIGIN - Yes, it will. Drive it in strong.

(LEARY drives blade in door frame with all his force)

LEARY - 'E'll have to find us 'ere.

CRAIGIN - Yes—and he won't either—we'll go on and do 'im up. (Going to door)

LARRABEE - No, you won't.

(Men stop. Pause.)

I'll see him first, if you please.

(CRAIGIN and LARRABEE facing each other savagely an instant well down stage.)

McTAGUE - Them was orders, Craigin.

LEARY - So it was.

McTAGUE - There might be time to get back in the passage. (He listens at door and cautiously looks off—turns back into room.) They ain't got up one flight yet.

LEARY - Quick then. (Moving toward door.)

(McTAGUE, LEARY and CRAIGIN go out. Door does not close. LARRABEE glances at door anxiously. Makes a quick dash up to it, and forces knife in with all his strength. Quickly pulls off coat and hat, throwing them on boxes, and sits quietly chewing an end of cigar. Enter SHERLOCK HOLMES at door, walking easily as though on some ordinary business.)

(Stop music.)

HOLMES - (seeing the apartment with a glance as he enters and Pausing, disappointed. His little laugh, with no smile) How the devil is it that you crooks always manage to hit on the same places for your scoundrelly business? (Chuckles of amusement.) Well! I certainly thought, after all this driving about in a closed cab you'd show me something new.

LARRABEE - (looking up nonchalantly) Seen it before, have you?

HOLMES - (standing still) Well, I should think so! (Moves easily about recalling dear old times.) I nabbed a friend of yours in this place while he was trying to drop himself out of that window. Ned Colvin, the cracksman.

LARRABEE - Colvin. I never heard of him before.

HOLMES - No? Ha! ha! Well, you certainly never heard of him after. A brace of counterfeiters used these regal chambers in the spring of '90. One of them hid in the cupboard. We pulled him out by the heels.

LARRABEE - (trying to get in on the nonchalance) Ah! Did you? And the other?

HOLMES - The other? He was more fortunate.

LARRABEE - Ah—he got away, I suppose.

HOLMES - Yes, he got away. We took his remains out through that door to the street. (Indicating door.)

LARRABEE - Quite interesting. (Drawled a little—looks at end of his cigar.)

(HOLMES is looking about.)

Times have changed since then.

(HOLMES darts a lightning glance at LARRABEE. Instantly easy again and glancing about as before.)

HOLMES - (dropping down near LARRABEE) So they have, Mr. Larrabee —so they have. (A little confidentially.) Then it was only cracksmen, counterfeiters, and petty swindlers of various kinds— Now —(Pause, looking at LARRABEE.)

(LARRABEE turns and looks at HOLMES.)

LARRABEE - Well? What now?

HOLMES - Well—(Mysteriously.) Between you and me, Larrabee —we've heard some not altogether agreeable rumors; rumours of some pretty shady work not far from here—a murder or two of a very peculiar kind—and I've always had a suspicion—(Stops. Sniffs very delicately. Motionless pause. Nods ominously to LARRABEE, who is looking about, and gets over towards window. When within reach he runs his hand lightly along the frame) My surmise was correct—it is.

LARRABEE - (turning to HOLMES) It is what?

HOLMES - Caulked.

LARRABEE - What does that signify to us?

HOLMES - Nothing to us, Mr. Larrabee, nothing to us, but it might signify a good deal to some poor devil who's been caught in this trap.

LARRABEE - Well if it's nothing to us suppose we leave it and get to business. My time is limited.

HOLMES - Quite so, of course. I should have realized that reflections could not possibly appeal to you. But it so happens I take a deep interest in anything that pertains to what are known as the criminal classes and this same interest makes me rather curious to know—(looking straight at LARRABEE, who looks up at him)—how you happened to select such a singularly gruesome place for an ordinary business transaction.

LARRABEE (looking at HOLMES across the table) I selected this places Mr. Holmes, because I thought you might not be disposed to take such liberties here as you practised in my own house last night.

HOLMES - Quite so, quite so. (Looks innocently at LARRABEE.) But why not?

(They look at one another an instant.)

LARRABEE - (significantly) You might not feel quite so much at home.

HOLMES - Oh—ha! (A little laugh.) You've made a singular miscalculation. I feel perfectly at home, Mr. Larrabee! Perfectly! (He seats himself at table in languid and leisurely manner, takes cigar from pocket and lights it.)

LARRABEE - (looks at him an instant) Well, I'm very glad to hear it.

(LARRABEE now takes out the counterfeit package of papers, etc., and tosses it on the table before them. HOLMES looks on floor slightly by light of match, unobserved by LARRABEE.)

Here is the little packet which is the object of this meeting. (He glances at HOLMES to see effect of its production.)

(HOLMES looks at it calmly as he smokes.)

I haven't opened it yet, but Miss Faulkner tells me everything is there.

HOLMES - Then there is no need of opening it, Mr. Larrabee.

LARRABEE - Oh, well—I want to see you satisfied.

HOLMES - That is precisely the condition in which you now behold me. Miss Faulkner is a truthful young lady. Her word is sufficient.

LARRABEE - Very well. Now what shall we say, Mr. Holmes? (Pause.) Of course, we want a pretty large price for this. Miss Faulkner is giving up everything. She would not be satisfied unless the result justified it.

HOLMES - (pointedly) Suppose, Mr. Larrabee, that as Miss Faulkner knows nothing whatever about this affair, we omit her name from the discussion.

(Slight pause of two seconds.)

LARRABEE - Who told you she doesn't know?

HOLMES - You did. Every look, tone, gesture—everything you have said and done since I have been in this room has informed me that she has never consented to this transaction. It is a little speculation of your own. (Tapping his fingers on end of table.)

LARRABEE - Ha! (Sneer.) I suppose you think you can read me like a book.

HOLMES - No—like a primer.

LARRABEE - Well, let that pass. How much'll you give?

HOLMES - A thousand pounds.

LARRABEE - I couldn't take it.

HOLMES - What do you ask?

LARRABEE - Five thousand.

HOLMES - (shakes head) I couldn't give it.

LARRABEE - Very well—(Rises.) We've had all this trouble for nothing. (As if about to put up the packet.)

HOLMES - (leaning back in chair and remonstrating) Oh—don't say that, Mr. Larrabee! To me the occasion has been doubly interesting. I have not only had the pleasure of meeting you again but I have also availed myself of the opportunity of making observations regarding this place which may not come amiss.

(LARRABEE looks at HOLMES contemptuously. He places chair under table.)

LARRABEE - Why, I've been offered four thousand for this little—

HOLMES - Why didn't you take it?

LARRABEE - Because I intend to get more.

HOLMES - That's too bad.

LARRABEE - If they offered four thousand they'll give five.

HOLMES - They won't give anything.

LARRABEE - Why not?

HOLMES - They've turned the case over to me.

LARRABEE - Will you give three thousand?

HOLMES - (rising) Mr. Larrabee, strange as it may appear, my time is limited as well as yours. I have brought with me the sum of One thousand pounds, which is all that I wish to pay. If it is your desire to sell at this figure kindly appraise me of the fact at once. If not, permit me to wish you a very good evening.

(Pause. LARRABEE looks at him.)

LARRABEE - (after the pause glances nervously round once, fearing he heard something) Go on! (Tosses packet on table.) You can have them. It's too small a matter to haggle over.

(HOLMES reseats himself at once, back of table, and takes wallet from his pocket, from which he produces a bunch of bank notes. LARRABEE stands watching him with glittering eye. HOLMES counts out ten one hundred pound notes and lays the remainder of the notes on the table with elbow on them, while he counts the first over again.)

(Sneeringly.) Oh—I thought you said you had brought just a thousand.

HOLMES - (not looking up; counting the notes) I did. This is it.

LARRABEE - You brought a trifle more, I see.

HOLMES - (counting notes) Quite so. I didn't say I hadn't brought any more.

LARRABEE - Ha! (Sneers.) You can do your little tricks when it comes to it, can't you?

HOLMES - It depends on who I'm dealing with. (Hands LARRABEE one thousand pounds in notes.)

(LARRABEE takes money and keeps a close watch at same time on the remaining pile of notes lying at HOLMES' left. HOLMES, after handing the notes to LARRABEE, lays cigar he was smoking on the table, picks up packet which he puts in his pocket with his right hand, and is almost at the same time reaching with his left hand for the notes he placed upon the table when LARRABEE makes a Sudden lunge and snatches the pile of bank notes, jumping back On the instant. HOLMES springs to his feet at the same time.)

Now I've got you where I want you, Jim Larrabee! You've been so cunning and so cautious and so wise, we couldn't find a thing to hold you for – but this little slip will get you in for robbery—

LARRABEE - Oh! You'll have me in, will you? (Short sneering laugh.) What are your views about being able to get away from here yourself?

HOLMES - I do not anticipate any particular difficulty.

LARRABEE - (significantly) Perhaps you'll change your mind about that.

HOLMES - Whether I change my mind or not, I certainly shall leave this place, and your arrest will shortly follow.

LARRABEE - My arrest? Ha, ha! Robbery, eh—Why, even if you got away from here you haven't got a witness. Not a witness to your name.

HOLMES - (slowly backing, keeping his eyes sharply on LARRABEE as he does so) I'm not so sure of that, Mr. Larrabee!—Do you usually fasten that door with a knife? (Pointing toward door with left arm and hand, but eyes on LARRABEE.)

(LARRABEE turns front as if bewildered. Tableau an instant. Very faint moan from within cupboard. HOLMES listens motionless an instant, then makes quick dash to door and seizing knife wrenches it out and flings it on the floor. LARRABEE seeing HOLMES start toward door of cupboard springs up to head him off)

LARRABEE - Come away from that door.

(But HOLMES has the door torn open and ALICE FAULKNER out before LARRABEE gets near.)

HOLMES - Stand back! (Turning to LARRABEE, supporting ALICE at same time.) You contemptible scoundrel! What does this mean!

LARRABEE - I'll show you what it means cursed quick. (Taking a step or two, blows the little silver whistle attached to his watch chain.)

HOLMES - (untying ALICE quickly) I'm afraid you're badly hurt Miss Faulkner.

(Enter CRAIGIN. He stands there a moment near door, watching HOLMES. He makes a signal with hand to others outside door and then moves noiselessly. McTAGUE enters noiselessly, and remains a little behind CRAIGIN below door. ALICE shakes her head quickly, thinking of what she sees, and tries to call HOLMES attention to CRAIGIN and McTAGUE.)

ALICE - No!—Mr. Holmes. (Pointing to CRAIGIN and McTAGUE.)

HOLMES (glances round) Ah, Craigin—delighted to see you.

(CRAIGIN gives slight start.)

And you too McTague. I infer from your presence here at this particular juncture that I am not dealing with Mr. Larrabee alone.

LARRABEE - Your inference is quite correct, Mr. Holmes.

HOLMES - It is not difficult to imagine who is at the bottom of such a conspiracy as this.

(CRAIGIN begins to steal across noiselessly. McTAGUE remains before door, HOLMES turns to ALICE again.)

I hope you're beginning to feel a little more yourself, Miss Faulkner —because we shall leave here very soon.

ALICE - (who has been shrinking from the sight of CRAIGIN and McTAGUE) Oh yes—do let us go, Mr. Holmes.

CRAIGIN - (low, deep voice, intense) You'll 'ave to wait a bit, Mr. 'Olmes. We 'ave a little matter of business we'd like to talk over.

(HOLMES turning to CRAIGIN.)

(Enter LEARY and glides up side in the shadow and begins to move towards HOLMES. In approaching from corner he glides behind door of cupboard as it stands open and from there down on HOLMES at cue. As HOLMES turns to CRAIGIN, ALICE leans against wall of cupboard .)

HOLMES - All right, Craigin, I'll see you to-morrow morning in your cell at Bow Street.

CRAIGIN - (threateningly) Werry sorry sir but I cawn't wait till morning Its got to be settled to night.

HOLMES (looks at CRAIGIN an instant) All right, Craigin, we'll settle it to-night.

CRAIGIN - It's so werry himportant, Mr. 'Olmes—so werry important indeed that you'll 'ave to 'tend to it now.

(At this instant ALICE sees LEARY approaching rapidly from behind and screams. HOLMES turns, but LEARY is upon him at the same time. There is a very short struggle and HOLMES throws LEARY violently off, but LEARY has got HOLMES' revolver. As they struggle ALICE steps back to side of room up stage. A short deadly pause. HOLMES motionless, regarding the men. ALICE'S back against wall. After the pause LEARY begins to revive.)

(Low voice to LEARY.) 'Ave you got his revolver?

LEARY - (showing revolver) 'Ere it is. (Getting slowly to his feet.)

HOLMES - (recognizing LEARY in the dim light) Ah, Leary! It is a pleasure indeed. It needed only your blithe personality to make the party complete. (Sits and writes rapidly on pocket pad, pushing lamp away a little and picking up cigar which he had left on the table, and which he keeps in his mouth as he writes.) There is only one other I could wish to welcome here, and that is the talented author of this midnight carnival. We shall have him however, by to- morrow night.

CRAIGIN - Though 'e ain't 'ere, Mr. 'Olmes, 'e gave me a message for yer. 'E presented his koindest compliments wished yer a pleasant trip across.

HOLMES - (writing—cigar in mouth) That's very kind of him, I'm sure. (Writes.)

LARRABEE - (sneeringly) You're writing your will, I suppose?

HOLMES (writing—with quick glances at the rest) No (Shakes head.) Only a brief description of one or two of you gentlemen for the police. We know the rest.

LEARY - And when will you give it 'em, Mr. 'Olmes?

HOLMES (writes) In nine or nine and a half minutes, Leary.

LARRABEE - Oh, you expect to leave here in nine minutes, eh?

HOLMES - No. (Writing.) In one. It will take me eight minutes to find a policeman. This is a dangerous neighbourhood.

LARRABEE - Well, when you're ready to start, let us know.

HOLMES - (rising and putting pad in pocket) I'm ready (Buttoning up coat.)

(CRAIGIN. McTAGUE and LEARY suddenly brace themselves for action, and stand ready to make a run for HOLMES. LARRABEE also is ready to join in the struggle if necessary. HOLMES moves backward from table a little to ALICE —she drops down a step towards HOLMES)

CRAIGIN - Wait a bit. You'd better listen to me, Mr. 'Olmes. We're going to tie yer down nice and tight to the top o' that table.

HOLMES - Well, by Jove! I don't think you will, That's my idea, you know.

CRAIGIN - An' you'll save yourself a deal of trouble if ye submit quiet and easy like—because if ye don't ye moight get knocked about a bit –

ALICE - (under her breath) Oh—Mr. Holmes! (Coming closer to HOLMES.)

LARRABEE - (to ALICE) Come away from him! Come over here if you don't want to get hurt.

(Love music.)

HOLMES - (to ALICE, without looking round, but reaching her with left hand) My child, if you don't want to get hurt, don't leave me for a second.

(ALICE moves closer to HOLMES.)

LARRABEE - Aren't you coming?

ALICE - (breathlessly) No!

CRAIGIN - You'd better look out, Miss—he might get killed.

ALICE - Then you can kill me too.

(HOLMES makes a quick turn to her, with sudden exclamation under breath. For an instant only he looks in her face—then a quick turn back to CRAIGIN and men.)

HOLMES - (low voice—not taking eyes from men before him) I'm afraid you don't mean that, Miss Faulkner.

ALICE - Yes, I do.

HOLMES - (eyes on men—though they shift about rapidly, but never toward ALICE) No. (Shakes head a trifle.) You would not say it —at another time or place.

ALICE - I would say it anywhere—always.

(Music stops.)

CRAIGIN - So you'll 'ave it out with us, eh?

HOLMES - Do you imagine for one moment, Craigin, that I won't have it out with you?

CRAIGIN - Well then—I'll 'ave to give you one—same as I did yer right-'and man this afternoon. (Approaching HOLMES.)

HOLMES - (to ALICE without turning—intense, rapid) Ah!

(CRAIGIN stops dead.)

You heard him say that. Same as he did my right-hand man this afternoon.

ALICE - (under breath) Yes! yes!

HOLMES - Don't forget that face. (Pointing to CRAIGIN.) In three days I shall ask you to identify it in the prisoner's dock.

CRAIGIN - (enraged) Ha! (Turning away as if to hide his face.)

HOLMES - (very sharp—rapid) Yes—and the rest of you with him. You surprise me, gentlemen— thinking you're sure of anybody in this room, and never once taking the trouble to look at that window. If you wanted to make it perfectly safe, you should have had those missing bars put in.

(HOLMES whispers something to ALICE, indicating her to make for door.)

(Music till end of Act.)

(CRAIGIN, LEARY, McTAGUE and LARRABEE make very slight move and say "Eh?" but instantly at tension again, and all motionless, ready to spring on HOLMES. HOLMES and ALICE motionless, facing them. This is held an instant.)

LARRABEE - Bars or no bars, you're not going to get out of here as easy as you expect.

(HOLMES moves easily down near table.)

HOLMES - There are so many ways, Mr. Larrabee, I hardly know which to choose.

CRAIGIN - (louder—advancing) Well, you'd better choose quick —I can tell you that.

HOLMES - (sudden—strong—sharp) I'll choose at once, Mr. Craigin—and my choice—(quickly seizing chair) —falls on this. (On the word he brings the chair down upon the lamp frightful crash, extinguishing light instantly.)

(Every light out. Only the glow of HOLMES' cigar remains where he stands at the table. He at once begins to move toward window keeping cigar so that it will show to men and to front.)

CRAIGIN - (loud sharp voice to others) Trace 'im by the cigar. (Moving at once toward window.) Follow the cigar.

LARRABEE - Look out. He's going for the window.

(LEARY goes quickly to window. McTAGUE goes and is ready by safety lamp. HOLMES quickly fixes cigar in a crack or joint at side of window so that it is still seen—smash of the window glass is heard. Instantly glides across, well up stage, and down side to the door where he finds ALICE. On crash of window CRAIGIN and LEARY give quick shout of exclamation – they spring up stage toward the light of cigar—sound of quick scuffle and blows in darkness.)

LARRABEE - Get that light.

CRAIGIN - (clear and distinct) The safety lamp. Where is it?

(Make this shout for lantern very strong and audible to front. McTAGUE kicks over box which concealed the safety lamp—lights up. HOLMES and ALICE at door. ALICE just going out.)

HOLMES - (turning at door and pointing to window) You'll find that cigar in a crevice by the window.

(All start towards HOLMES with exclamations, oaths, etc. He makes quick exit with ALICE and slams door after him. Sounds of heavy bolts outside sliding quickly into place, and heavy bars dropping into position. CRAIGIN, McTAGUE and LEARY rush against door and make violent efforts to open it. After the first excited effort they turn quickly back. As McTAGUE crosses he throws safely lamp on table. LARRABEE, who has stopped near when he saw door closed, turns front with a look of hatred on his face and mad with rage.)

CURTAIN

ACT IV

SCENE.—DR. WATSON'S house in Kensington. The consulting room. Oak panelling. Solid furniture. Wide double-doors opening to the hall and street door. Door communicating with doctor's inner medicine room. Another door, center, opens to private hallway of house. The windows are supposed to open at side of house upon an area which faces the street. These windows have shades or blinds on rollers which can quickly be drawn down. At the opening of the Act they are down, so that no one could see into the room from the street.

There is a large operating chair with high back, cushions, etc. Music for curtain, which stops an instant before rise.

DR. WATSON is seated behind his desk and MRS. SMEEDLEY, a seedy- looking middle-aged woman, is seated in the chair next to the desk with a medicine bottle in her hand.

WATSON - Be careful to make no mistake about the medicine. If she's no better to-morrow I'll call. You will let me know, of course.

MRS. SMEEDLEY - Oh yes, indeed I will. Good evening, sir.

WATSON - Good night, Mrs. Smeedley.

(MRS. SMEEDLEY goes out. Sound of door closing heard after she is off. Pause. The doctor turns to his desk, and ringing bell, busies himself with papers.)

(Enter PARSONS—a servant.)

Parsons!

(PARSONS comes a little towards WATSON.)

(Lower voice.) That woman who just left—do you know her?

PARSONS - (trying to recollect) I can't say as I recollect 'avin' seen 'er before. Was there anything—?

WATSON - Oh no! Acted a little strange, that's all. I thought I saw her looking about the hall before she went out.

PARSONS - Yes sir, she did give a look. I saw that myself, sir.

WATSON - (after an instant's thought) Oh well—I dare say it was nothing. Is there anyone waiting, Parsons?

PARSONS - There's one person in the waiting-room, sir—a gentleman.

WATSON - (looks at watch) I'll see him, but I've only a short time left. If any more come you must send them over to Doctor Anstruther. I spoke to him this afternoon about taking my cases. I have an important appointment at nine.

PARSONS - Very well, sir. Then you'll see this gentleman, sir?

WATSON - Yes.

(PARSONS goes out. Short pause. WATSON busy at desk. PARSONS opens door and shows in SID PRINCE. He comes in a little way and pauses. PARSONS all through this Act closes the door after his exit, or after showing anyone in. WATSON looks up.)

PRINCE - (speaking in the most dreadful husky whisper) Good evenin', sir!

WATSON - Good evening. (Indicating chair.) Pray be seated.

PRINCE - (same voice all through) Thanks, I don't mind if I do. (Coughs, then sits in chair near desk.)

WATSON - (looking at him with professional interest) What seems to be the trouble?

PRINCE - Throat, sir. (Indicating his throat to assist in making himself understood.) Most dreadful sore throat.

WATSON - Sore throat, eh? (Glancing about for an instrument.)

PRINCE - Well, I should think it is. It's the most 'arrowing thing I ever 'ad! It pains me that much to swallow that I—

WATSON - Hurts you to swallow, does it? (Finding and picking up an instrument on the desk.)

PRINCE - Indeed it does. Why, I can 'ardly get a bit of food down.

(WATSON rises and goes to cabinet, pushes gas burner out into position and lights it.)

WATSON - Just step this way a moment, please. (PRINCE rises and goes up to WATSON, who adjusts reflector over eye, etc. He has an instrument in his hand which he wipes with a napkin.) Now, mouth open—wide as possible. (PRINCE opens mouth and WATSON places tongue holder on his tongue.) That's it. (Picks up dentist's mirror and warms it over gas burner.)

PRINCE - (WATSON is about to examine throat when PRINCE sees instrument and is a trifle alarmed) Eh!

(Business of WATSON putting in tongue holder and looking down PRINCES throat—looking carefully this way and that)

WATSON - Say "Ah!"

PRINCE - (husky voice) Ah! (Steps away and places handkerchief to mouth as if the attempt to say Ah! hurt him)

(WATSON discontinues, and takes instrument out of PRINCE'S mouth.)

WATSON - (a slight incredulity in his manner) Where do you feel this pain?

PRINCE - (indicating with his finger) Just about there, doctor. Inside about there.

WATSON - That's singular. I don't find anything wrong. (gas burner back to usual position—and placing instrument on cabinet.)

PRINCE - You may not foind anything wrong, but I feel it wrong. If you would only give me something to take away this awful agony.

WATSON - That's nothing. It'll pass away in a few hours. (Reflectively.) Singular thing it would have affected your voice in this way. Well, I'll give you a gargle—it may help you a little.

PRINCE - Yes—if you only would, doctor.

(WATSON goes into surgery PRINCE watching him like a cat. Music. Dramatic agitato, very pp. WATSON does not close the door of the room, but pushes it part way so that it is open about a foot. PRINCE moves toward door, watching WATSON through it. Stops near door. Seems to watch for his chance, for he suddenly turns and goes quickly down and runs up blinds of both windows and moves back quickly, watching WATSON through the door again. Seeing that he still has time to spare, he goes to centre door and opens it, looking and listening off. Distant sound of a when door is open which stops when it is closed. PRINCE quickly turns back and goes off a little way at centre door, leaving it open so that he is seen peering up above and listening. Turns to come back, but just at the door he sees WATSON coming on and stops. WATSON suddenly enters and sees PRINCE in centre door and stops, with a bottle in his hand, and looks at PRINCE.)

(Music stops.)

WATSON - What are you doing there?

PRINCE - Why, nothing at all, doctor. I felt such a draught on the back o' my neck, don't yer know, that I opened the door to see where it came from!

(WATSON goes down and rings bell on his desk, placing bottle on papers. Pause. Enter PARSONS.)

WATSON - Parsons, show this man the shortest way to the street door and close the door after him.

PRINCE - But, doctor, ye don't understand.

WATSON - I understand quite enough. Good evening.

PRINCE - Yer know, the draught plays hell with my throat, sir—and seems to affect my—

WATSON - Good evening. (He sits and pays no further attention to PRINCE.)

PARSONS - This way, sir, if you please.

PRINCE - I consider that you've treated me damned outrageous, that's wot I do, and ye won't hear the last of this very soon.

PARSONS - (approaching him) Come, none o' that now. (Takes PRINCE by the arm.)

PRINCE - (as he walks toward door with PARSONS, turns head back and speaks over his shoulder, shouting out in his natural voice) Yer call yerself a doctor an' treats sick people as comes to see yer this 'ere way. (Goes out with PARSONS and continues talking until slam of door outside.) Yer call yerself a doctor! A bloomin' foine doctor you are! (Etc.)

(PARSONS has forced PRINCE out by the arm during foregoing speech. Door closes after PRINCE. Sound of outside door closing follows shortly. WATSON, after short pause, looks round room, not observing that window shades are up. He rings bell. Enter PARSONS)

WATSON - (rises and gathers up a few things as if to go) I shall be at Mr. Holmes's in Baker Street. If there's anything special, you'll know where to send for me. The appointment was for nine. (Looks at watch.) It's fifteen minutes past eight now—I'm going to walk over.

PARSONS - Very well, sir.

(Bell of outside door rings. PARSONS looks at WATSON, who shakes his head.)

WATSON - No. I won't see any more to-night. They must go to Doctor Anstruther.

PARSONS - Yes, sir. (He starts towards door to answer bell.)

(WATSON looks and sees blinds up.)

WATSON - Parsons! (PARSONS turns.) Why aren't those blinds down?

PARSONS - They was down a few minutes ago, sir!

WATSON - That's strange! Well, you'd better pull them down now.

PARSONS - Yes, sir.

(Bell rings twice as PARSONS pulls second blind down. He goes out to answer bell. Pause. Then enter PARSONS in a peculiar manner.)

If you please, sir, it isn't a patient at all, sir.

WATSON - Well, what is it?

PARSONS - A lady sir—(WATSON looks up)—and she wants to see you most particular, sir!

WATSON - What does she want to see me about?

PARSONS - She didn't say sir. Only she said it was of the hutmost himportance to 'er, if you could see 'er, sir.

WATSON - Is she there in the hall?

PARSONS - Yes sir.

WATSON - Very well—I was going to walk for the exercise—I can take a cab.

PARSONS - Then you'll see the lady, sir.

WATSON - Yes. (PARSONS turns to go. WATSON continues his preparations.) And call a cab for me at the same time—have it wait.

PARSONS - Yes, sir.

(PARSONS goes out. Pause. PARSONS appears, ushering in a lady – and goes when she has entered. Enter MADGE LARRABEE. Her manner is entirely different from that of the former scenes. She is an impetuous gushing society lady with trouble on her mind)

MADGE - (as she comes in) Ah! Doctor—it's awfully good of you to see me. I know what a busy man you must be but I'm in such trouble —oh, it's really too dreadful—You'll excuse my troubling you in this way, won't you?

WATSON - Don't speak of it, madam.

MADGE - Oh, thank you so much! For it did look frightful my coming in like this—but I'm not alone—oh no!—I left my maid in the cab—I'm Mrs. H. de Witte Seaton—(Trying to find card- case.) Dear me—I didn't bring my card-case—or if I did I lost it.

WATSON - Don't trouble about a card, Mrs. Seaton. (With gesture to indicate chair.)

MADGE - Oh, thank you. (Sitting as she continues to talk.) You don't know what I've been through this evening—trying to find some one who could tell me what to do. (WATSON sits in chair at desk.) It's something that's happened, doctor—it has just simply happened – I know that it wasn't his fault! I know it!

WATSON - Whose fault?

MADGE - My brother's—my poor, dear, youngest brother—he couldn't have done such a thing, he simply couldn't and—

WATSON - Such a thing as what, Mrs. Seaton?

MADGE - As to take the plans of our defences at Gibraltar from the Admiralty Offices. They think he stole them, doctor—and they've arrested him for it—you see, he works there. He was the only one who knew about them in the whole office—because they trusted him so. He was to make copies and—Oh, doctor, it's really too dreadful! (Overcome, she takes out her handkerchief and wipes her eyes. This must all be perfectly natural, and not in the least particular overdone.)

WATSON - I'm very sorry, Mrs. Seaton—

MADGE - (mixed up with sobs) Oh, thank you so much! They said you were Mr. Holmes's friend—several people told me that, several – they advised me to ask you where I could find him—and everything depends on it, doctor—everything.

WATSON - Holmes, of course. He's just the one you want.

MADGE - That's it! He's just the one—and there's hardly any time left! They'll take my poor brother away to prison to-morrow! (Shows signs of breaking down again.)

WATSON - There, there, Mrs. Seaton—pray control yourself.

MADGE - (choking down sobs) Now what would you advise me to do?

WATSON - I'd go to Mr. Holmes at once.

MADGE - But I've been. I've been and he wasn't there!

WATSON - You went to his house?

MADGE - Yes—in Baker Street. That's why I came to you! They said he might be here!

WATSON - No—he isn't here! (Turns away slightly)

(MADGE looks deeply discouraged)

MADGE - But don't you expect him some time this evening?

WATSON - No (Shaking head) There's no possibility of his coming —so far as I know.

MADGE - But couldn't you get him to come? (Pause) It would be such a great favour to me—I'm almost worn out with going about—and with this dreadful anxiety! If you could get word to him—(sees that WATSON is looking at her strangely and sharply)—to come.

(Brief pause)

WATSON - (rising—rather hard voice) I could not get him to come madam. And I beg you to excuse me I am going out myself – (looks at watch)—on urgent business. (Rings bell.)

MADGE - (rising) Oh certainly! Don t let me detain you! And you think I had better call at his house again?

WATSON - (coldly) That will be the wisest thing to do.

MADGE - Oh, thank you so much. (Extends her hand.) You don t know how you've encouraged me!

(WATSON withdraws his hand as he still looks at her. Enter PARSONS He stands at door)

Well—good night doctor

(WATSON simply bows coldly. MADGE turns to go. The crash of a capsizing vehicle followed by excited shouts of men is heard. This effect must be as if outside the house with doors closed and not close at hand. MADGE stops suddenly on hearing the crash and all shouts. WATSON looks at PARSONS.)

WATSON - What's that Parsons?

PARSONS - I really can't say sir but it sounded to me like a haccident.

MADGE - (turning to WATSON) Oh dear! I do hope it isn't anything serious! It affects me terribly to know that anyone is hurt.

WATSON - Probably nothing more than a broken-down cab. See what it is, Parsons.

(Bell and knock. MADGE turns and looks toward door again, anxiously PARSONS turns to go. Sudden vigorous ringing of door bell, followed by the sound of a knocker violently used.)

PARSONS - There's the bell, sir! There's somebody 'urt, sir, an' they're a- wantin' you!

WATSON - Well, don't allow anybody to come in! (Looks at watch.) I have no more time. (Hurriedly gathers papers up.)

PARSONS - Very well, sir. (Goes leaving door open.)

(MADGE turns from looking off at door, and looks at WATSON anxiously. Looks toward door again.)

MADGE - But they're coming in, doctor. (Retreats backward.)

WATSON - (moving toward door) Parsons! Parsons!

(Sound of voices. Following speeches outside are not in rotation, but jumbled together, so that it is all over very quickly.)

VOICE - (outside) We 'ad to bring 'im in, man.

VOICE - (outside) There's nowhere else to go!

PARSONS - (outside) The doctor can't see anybody.

VOICE - (outside) Well let the old gent lay 'ere awhile can't yer. It's common decency. Wot 'ave yer got a red lamp 'angin' outside yer bloomin' door for?

VOICE - (outside) Yes! yes! let him stay.

(Enter PARSONS at door. Door closes and noise stops.)

PARSONS - They would bring 'im in, sir. It's an old gentleman as was 'urt a bit w'en the cab upset!

MADGE - Oh!

(Sound of groans, etc. outside, and the old gentleman whining out complaints and threats.)

WATSON - Let them put him here. (Indicating operating chair.) And send at once for Doctor Anstruther.

PARSONS - Yes, sir!

WATSON - Help him in Parsons.

(PARSONS goes out)

MADGE - Oh doctor isn't it frightful.

WATSON - (turning to centre door) Mrs Seaton if you will be so good as to step this way, you can reach the hall, by taking the first door to your left.

MADGE - (hesitating) But I—I may be of some use doctor.

WATSON - (with a trifle of impatience) None whatever (Holds door open.)

MADGE - But doctor—I must see the poor fellow—I haven't the power to go!

WATSON (facing MADGE) Madam, I believe you have some ulterior motive in coming here! You will kindly—

(Enter at door a white-haired old gentleman in black clerical clothes, white tie, etc., assisted by PARSONS and the DRIVER. He limps as though his leg were hurt. His coat is soiled. His hat is soiled as if it had rolled in the street. MADGE has retired above desk and watches old gent closely from there without moving. WATSON turns toward the party as they come in.)

HOLMES (as he comes in) Oh, oh! (He limps so that he hardly touches his right foot to floor)

PARSONS (as he helps HOLMES in) This way, sir! Be careful of the sill, sir! That's it. (Etc.)

DRIVER - (as he comes in, and also beginning outside before entrance) Now we'll go in 'ere. You'll see the doctor an' it'll be all right.

HOLMES - No, it won't be all right.

DRIVER - It was a haccident. You cawn't 'elp a haccident.

HOLMES - Yes, you can.

DRIVER - He was on the wrong side of the street. I turned hup — (Etc.)

PARSONS - Now over to this chair. (Indicating operating chair).

HOLMES - (pushing back and trying to stop at the desk chair) No, I'll sit here.

PARSONS - No, this is the chair, sir.

HOLMES - Don't I know where I want to sit?

DRIVER - (impatiently) You'll sit 'ere. (They lead him up to operating chair.)

DRIVER - (as they lead him up) Now, the doctor'll have a look at ye. 'Ere's the doctor.

HOLMES - That isn't a doctor.

DRIVER - It is a doctor. (Seeing WATSON.) 'Ere, doctor, will you just come and have a look at this old gent? (HOLMES trying to stop him.) He's hurt 'isself a little, an'—an'—

HOLMES - (trying to stop DRIVER) Wait, wait, wait!

DRIVER - Well, well?

HOLMES - (still standing back to audience and turned to DRIVER) Are you the driver?

DRIVER - Yes, I'm the driver.

HOLMES - Well, I'll have you arrested for this.

DRIVER - Arrested?

HOLMES - Arrested, arrested, arrested!

DRIVER - You cawn't arrest me.

HOLMES - I can't, but somebody else can.

DRIVER - 'Ere, 'ere. (Trying to urge HOLMES to chair.)

HOLMES - You are a very disagreeable man! You are totally uninformed on every subject! I wonder you are able to live in the same house with yourself.

(The DRIVER is trying to talk back and make HOLMES sit down. HOLMES turns suddenly on PARSONS. WATSON is trying to attract PARSONS' attention.)

Are you a driver?

PARSONS - No, sir!

HOLMES - Well, what are you?

PARSONS - I'm the butler, sir.

HOLMES - Butler! Butler!

DRIVER - He's the doctor's servant.

HOLMES - Who'd have such a looking butler as you! What fool would –

DRIVER - (turning HOLMES toward him roughly) He is the doctor's servant!

HOLMES - Who asked you who he was?

DRIVER - Never mind who asked me—I'm telling you.

HOLMES - Well, go and tell somebody else.

DRIVER - (trying to push HOLMES into chair) Sit down here. Sit down and be quiet

WATSON - (to PARSONS) Have a cab ready for me. I must see if he's badly hurt.

PARSONS - Yes, sir. (Goes.)

HOLMES - (resisting) Quiet! quiet! Where's my hat? My hat! My hat!

DRIVER - Never mind your 'at.

HOLMES - I will mind my hat! and I hold you responsible—

DRIVER - There's your hat in your 'and.

HOLMES - (looks at hat) That isn't my hat! Here! (DRIVER trying to push him into chair.) You're responsible. (In chair.) I'll have you arrested. (Clinging to DRIVER'S coat tail as he tries to get away to door) Here come back (Choking with rage)

DRIVER - (first wrenching away coat from HOLMES' grasp at door) I cawn't stay around 'ere, you know! Some one'll pinching my cab. (Exit.)

HOLMES - (screaming after him) Then bring your cab in here. I want —(Lapses into groans and remonstrances.) Why didn't somebody stop him? These cabmen! What did he bring me in for? I know where I am, it's a conspiracy. I won't stay in this place. If I ever get out of here alive —(Etc.)

WATSON - (steps quickly to door, speaking off) Parsons—that man's number (quickly to old gent) Now sir if you'll be quiet for one moment, I'll have a look at you! (Crosses to end of cabinet as if to look for instrument.)

(MADGE advances near to the old gentleman, looking at him closely. She suddenly seems to be satisfied of something, backs away, and reaching out as if to get to the window and give signal, then coming face to face with WATSON as he turns, and smiling pleasantly at him. Business with glove. She begins to glide down stage, making a sweep around toward door as if to get out. She shows by her expression that she has recognized HOLMES, but is instantly herself again, thinking possibly that HOLMES is watch her, and she wishes to evade suspicion regarding her determination to get off at door. Quick as a flash the old gentleman springs to the door and stands facing her. She stops suddenly on finding him facing her, then wheels quickly about and goes rapidly across toward window)

HOLMES - (sharp) Don't let her get to that window.

(WATSON, who had moved up a little above windows, instantly springs before the windows. MADGE stops on being headed off in that direction.)

WATSON - Is that you, Holmes?

(MADGE stands motionless.)

HOLMES - Quite so. (Takes off his wig, etc.)

WATSON - What do you want me to do?

HOLMES - (easily) That's all, you've done it. Don't do anything more just now.

(MADGE gives a sharp look at them, then goes very slowly for a few steps and suddenly turns and makes a dash for centre door.)

WATSON - Look out, Holmes! She can get out that way. (A step or two up.)

(MADGE runs off. HOLMES is unmoved.)

HOLMES - I don't think so. (Saunters over to above WATSON'S desk.) Well, well, what remarkable weather we're having, doctor, eh? (Suddenly seeing cigarettes on desk.) Ah! I'm glad to see that you keep a few prescriptions carefully done up. (Picks up a cigarette and sits on desk.) Good for the nerves! (HOLMES finds matches and lights cigarette.) Have you ever observed, Watson, that those people are always making—

(Enter the DRIVER.)

FORMAN - (speaking at once—so as to break in on HOLMES) I've got her, sir!

(Very brief pause.)

WATSON - Good heavens! Is that Forman?

(HOLMES nods "Yes.")

HOLMES - Yes, that's Forman all right. Has Inspector Bradstreet Come with his men?

FORMAN - Yes, sir. One of 'em's in the hall there 'olding her. The others are in the kitchen garden. They came in over the back Wall from Mortimer Street.

HOLMES - One moment. (Sits in thought.) Watson, my dear fellow —(WATSON moves toward HOLMES at desk.) As you doubtless gather from the little episode that has just taken place we are making the arrests. The scoundrels are hot on my track. To get me out of the way is the one chance left to them—and I taking advantage of their mad pursuit to draw them where we quietly lay our hands on them—one by one. We've made a pretty good haul already—four last night in the gas chamber —seven this afternoon in various places, and one more just now, but I regret to say that up to this time the Professor himself has so far not risen to the bait.

WATSON - Where do you think he is now?

HOLMES - In the open streets—under some clever disguise – watching for a chance to get at me.

WATSON - And was this woman sent in here to—

HOLMES - Quite so. A spy—to let them know by some signal, probably at that window—(pointing)— if she found me in the house. And it has Just occurred to me that it might not be such a bad idea to try the Professor with that bait. Forman! (Motions him to come down.)

FORMAN - Yes, sir!

HOLMES - (voice lower) One moment (Business) Bring that Larrabee woman back here for a moment, and when I light a fresh cigarette —let go your hold on her—carelessly—as if your attention was attracted to something else. Get hold of her again when I tell you.

FORMAN - Very well sir.

(Goes quickly to re-enter bringing in MADGE LARRABEE. They stop. MADGE calm, but looks at HOLMES with the utmost hatred. Brief pause.)

HOLMES - My dear Mrs. Larrabee—(MADGE, who has looked away, turns to him angrily)—I took the liberty of having you brought in for a moment—(puffs cigarette, which he has nearly finished) —in order to convey to you in a few fitting words—my sincere sympathy in your rather—unpleasant—predicament,

MADGE - (hissing it out angrily between her teeth) It's a lie! It's a lie! There's no predicament.

HOLMES - Ah—I'm charmed to gather—from your rather forcible observation—that you do not regard it as such. Quite right, too. Our prisons are so well conducted now. Many consider them quite as comfortable as most of the hotels. Quieter and more orderly.

MADGE - How the prisons are conducted is no concern of mine! There is nothing they can hold me for—nothing.

HOLMES - Oh—to be sure. (Putting fresh cigarette in mouth.) There may be something in that. Still—it occurred to me that you might prefer to be near your unfortunate husband—eh? (Rises from table and goes to gas burner. Slight good-natured chuckle.) We hear a great deal about the heroic devotion of wives, and all that – (lights cigarette at gas)—rubbish. You know, Mrs. Larrabee, when we come right down to it—(FORMAN carelessly relinquishes his hold on MADGE'S arm, and seems to have his attention called to door. Stands as if listening to something outside. MADGE gives a quick glance about and at HOLMES who is lighting a cigarette at the gas, and apparently not noticing anything. She makes a sudden dash for the window, quickly snaps up blind and makes a rapid motion up and down before window with right hand—then turns quickly, facing HOLMES with triumphant defiance. HOLMES is still lighting cigarette.)

Many thanks. (To FORMAN.) That's all, Forman. Pick her up again.

(FORMAN at once goes to MADGE and turns her and waits in front of window—holding her right wrist.)

Doctor, would you kindly pull the blind down once more. I don't care to be shot from the street.

(WATSON instantly pulls down blind.)

(NOTE—Special care must be exercised regarding these window blinds. They must be made specially strong and solid, so that no failure to operate is possible.)

MADGE - (in triumph) Ah! It's too late.

HOLMES - Too late, eh? (Strolling a little.)

MADGE - The signal is given. You will hear from him soon.

HOLMES - It wouldn't surprise me at all.

(Door bell rings.)

(Voices of BILLY and PARSONS outside. Door at once opened, BILLY on a little way, but held back by PARSONS for an instant. He breaks away from PARSONS. All very quick, BILLY dressed as a street gamin and carrying a bunch of evening papers)

(As BILLY comes.) I think I shall hear from him now. (Shout.) Let—(BILLY stands panting)—him go, Parsons. Quick, Billy.

(BILLY comes close to HOLMES.)

BILLY - He's just come sir.

HOLMES - From where?

BILLY - The house across the street; he was in there a-watchin' these windows. He must 'ave seen something for he's just come out – (Breathlessly.) There was a cab waitin' in the street for the doctor —and he's changed places with the driver.

HOLMES - Where did the driver go?

BILLY - He slunk away in the dark, sir, but he ain't gone far, there's two or three more 'angin' about.

HOLMES - (slight motion of the head towards FORMAN) another driver to- night.

BILLY - They're all in it, sir, an' they're a-layin' to get you in that cab w'en you come out, sir! But don't you do it, sir!

HOLMES - On the contrary, sir, I'll have that new driver in here sir! Get out again quick, Billy, and keep your eyes on him!

BILLY - Yes, sir—thank you, sir! (Goes.)

HOLMES - Yes, sir! Watson, can you let me have a heavy portmanteau for a few moments—?

(MADGE now watching for another chance to get at the window.)

WATSON - Parsons—my large Gladstone—bring it here!

PARSONS - Yes, sir. (Goes out.)

WATSON - I'm afraid it's a pretty shabby looking—

(MADGE suddenly tries to break loose from FORMAN and attempt to make a dash for window. FORMAN turns and pulls her a step or two away. Slight pause.)

HOLMES - Many thanks, Mrs. Larrabee, but your first signal is all that we require. By it you informed your friend Moriarty that I was here in the house. You are now aware of the fact that he is impersonating a driver, and that it is my intention to have him in here. You wish to signal that there is danger. There is danger, Mrs. Larrabee, but we don't care to have you let him know it. Take her out, Forman, and make her comfortable and happy.

(FORMAN leads MADGE up to centre door as if to take her out. She pulls him to a stop and gives HOLMES a look of the most violent hatred.)

And by the way, you might tell the inspector to wait a few moments. I may send him another lot. You can't tell!

FORMAN - Come along now! (Takes her off)

(As MADGE is pulled up, she snaps her fingers in HOLMES'S face and goes off laughing hysterically.)

HOLMES - Fine woman!

(Enter PARSONS, carrying a large portmanteau or Gladstone valise.)

Put it down there. (Pointing down before him at floor.) Thank you so much.

(PARSONS puts portmanteau down as indicated.)

Parsons, you ordered a cab for the doctor a short time ago. It has been waiting, I believe.

PARSONS - Yes, sir, I think it 'as.

HOLMES - Be so good as to tell the driver, the one you'll now find there, to come in here and get a valise. See that he comes in himself When he comes tell him that's the one.

(PARSONS goes.)

WATSON - But surely he won't come in.

HOLMES - Surely he will! It's his only chance to get me into that cab! He'll take almost any risk for that. (Goes to above desk.) In times like this you should tell your man never to take the first cab that comes on a call—(smokes)—nor yet the second—the third may be safe!

WATSON - But in this case—

HOLMES - My dear fellow, I admit that in this case I have it to my advantage, but I speak for your future guidance.

(Music Melodramatic danger agitato very subdued)

(Door opens. PARSONS enters, pointing the portmanteau out to some one who is following.)

PARSONS - 'Ere it is—right in, this way.

HOLMES - (goes to WATSON above table. In rather a loud voice to WATSON) Well, good-bye, old fellow! (Shakes hands with him warmly and bringing him down left a little.) I'll write you from Paris— and I hope you'll keep me fully informed of the progress of events.

(MORIARTY enters in the disguise of a cabman and goes at once to valise which PARSONS points out, trying to hurry it through and keeping face away from HOLMES but fidgeting about, not touching valise. PARSONS goes out.)

(Speaks right on, apparently paying no attention to MORIARTY) As for these papers I'll attend to them personally. Here my man—(to MORIARTY)—just help me to tighten up these straps and bit – (He slides over to valise and kneels, pulling at strap, and MORIARTY bending over and doing same.) There are a few little things in this bag —(business)—that I wouldn't like to lose – (business)—and its Just as well to—Eh – (looking round for instant)—who's that at the window?

(MORIARTY quickly looks up without lifting hands from valise and at the same instant the snap of handcuffs is heard, and he springs up with the irons on his wrists, making two or three violent efforts to break loose. He then stands motionless. HOLMES drops into chair, a cigarette in his mouth. MORIARTY in rising knocks his hat off and stands facing audience.)

(Music stops.)

(In a very quiet tone.) Doctor, will you kindly strike the bell two or three times in rapid succession.

(WATSON steps to desk and gives several rapid strokes of the bell.)

Thanks!

(Enter FORMAN. FORMAN goes down to MORIARTY and fastens handcuffs which he has on his own wrists to chain attached to that of MORIARTY'S. This is held an instant—the two men looking at each other.)

Forman!

FORMAN - Yes, sir.

HOLMES - Got a man there with you?

FORMAN - Yes, sir, the inspector came in himself.

HOLMES - Ah—the inspector himself. We shall read graphic accounts in to-morrow's papers of a very difficult arrest he succeeded in making at Dr. Watson's house in Kensington. Take him out, Forman, and introduce him to the inspector—they'll be pleased to meet.

(FORMAN starts to force MORIARTY off MORIARTY hangs back and endeavours to get at HOLMES—a very slight struggle.)

Here! Wait! Let's see what he wants!

MORIARTY - (low voice to HOLMES) Do you imagine, Sherlock Holmes, that this is the end.

HOLMES - I ventured to dream that it might be.

MORIARTY - Are you quite sure the police will be able to hold me?

HOLMES - I am quite sure of nothing.

MORIARTY - Ah! (Slight pause.) I have heard that you are planning to take a little trip—you and your friend here—a little trip on the Continent.

HOLMES - And if I do?

MORIARTY - (a step to HOLMES) I shall meet you there. (Slight pause.)

HOLMES - That's all, Forman.

(FORMAN moves up to door, quietly with MORIARTY.)

MORIARTY - (stopping at door) I shall meet you there. You will Change your course—you will try to elude me—but whichever way you turn—there will be eyes that see and wires that tell. I shall meet you there—and you know it. You know it!—and you know it. (Goes with FORMAN.)

(Pause.)

HOLMES - Did you hear that, Watson?

WATSON - Yes—but surely you don't place any importance on such –

HOLMES - (stopping him with wave of hand) Oh! no importance. But I have a fancy that he spoke the truth.

WATSON - We'll give up the trip.

HOLMES - (a negative wave of the hand at WATSON) It would be quite the same. What matters it here or there—if it must come (Sits meditative)

WATSON - (calling) Parsons!

(PARSONS comes in WATSON points to the valise PARSONS removes it and goes.)

HOLMES - Watson, my dear fellow—(smokes)—it's too bad. Now that this is all over, I suppose you imagine that your room will no longer be required. Let me assure—let me assure you (voice trembles)—that the worst is yet to come.

WATSON - (stands in front of desk) The worst to—(Suddenly thinks of something. Pulls out watch hurriedly.) Why, heavens Holmes we have barely five minutes.

HOLMES - (looks up innocently at him) For what?

WATSON - To get to Baker Street—your rooms!

(HOLMES still looks at him.)

Your appointment with Sir Edward and the Count! They were to receive that packet of letters from you.

HOLMES - (nods assent) They're coming here.

(Pause. WATSON looking at HOLMES.)

WATSON - Here!

HOLMES - That is—if you will be so good as to permit it.

WATSON Certainly—but why not there?

HOLMES - The police wouldn't allow us inside the ropes.

WATSON - Police! Ropes!

HOLMES - Police—ropes—ladders—hose—crowds —engines—

WATSON - Why, you don't mean that—

HOLMES - (nods) Quite so—the devils have burned me out.

WATSON - Good heavens—burned you—

(Pause. HOLMES nods.)

Oh, that's too bad. What did you lose?

HOLMES - Everything!—everything! I'm so glad of it! I've had enough. This one thing—(right hand strong gesture of emphasis —he stops in midst of sentence—a frown upon his face as he thinks—then in a lower voice)—ends it! This one thing —that I shall do—here in a few moments—is the finish. (HOLMES rises.)

WATSON - You mean—Miss Faulkner?

(HOLMES nods slightly in affirmative without turning to WATSON.)

(Love music. Very pp.)

HOLMES - (turning suddenly to WATSON) Watson—she trusted me! She—clung to me! There were four to one against me! They said "Come here," I said "Stay close to me," and she did! She clung to me—I could feel her heart beating against mine—and I was playing a game! —(lower—parenthetical)—a dangerous game – but I was playing it!—It will be the same to-night! She'll be there —I'll be here! She'll listen—she'll believe—and she'll trust me—and I'll—be playing—a game. No more – I've had enough! It's my last case!

(WATSON has been watching him narrowly.)

Oh well! what does it matter? Life is a small affair at the most—a little while—a few sunrises and sunsets—the warm breath of a few summers—the cold chill of a few winters—(Looking down on floor a little way before him in meditation.) And then – (Pause.)

WATSON - And then—?

(HOLMES glances up at him. Upward toss of hand before speaking.)

HOLMES - And then.

(The music stops.)

WATSON - (going to HOLMES) My dear Holmes—I'm afraid that plan of—gaining her confidence and regard went a little further than you intended—

(HOLMES nods assent slightly)

HOLMES - (mutters after nodding) A trifle!

WATSON - For—her—or for you?

HOLMES - For her—(looks up at WATSON slowly)—and for me.

WATSON - (astonished. After an instant's pause) But—if you both love each other—

HOLMES - (putting hand on WATSON to stop him sharply) Sh—! Don't say it! (Pause.) You mustn't tempt me—with such a thought. That girl!—young—exquisite—just beginning her sweet life—I—seared, drugged, poisoned, almost at an end! No! no! I must cure her! I must stop it, now—while there's time! (Pause.) She's coming here.

WATSON - She won't come alone?

HOLMES - No, Térèse will be with her.

(HOLMES turns and goes to door to surgery, getting a book on the way, and placing it in the way of door closing. Turns to WATSON)

When she comes let her wait in that room. You can manage that, I'm quite sure.

WATSON - Certainly—Do you intend to leave that book there

HOLMES (nods "Yes") To keep that door from closing. She is to overhear.

WATSON - I see.

HOLMES - Sir Edward and the Count are very likely to become excited. I shall endeavour to make them so. You must not be alarmed old fellow.

(Bell of outside door rings off HOLMES and WATSON look at one another.)

(Going to centre door.) She may be there now. I'll go to your dressing- room, if you'll allow me, and brush away some of this dust.

WATSON - By all means! (Goes to door.) My wife is in the drawing- room. Do look in on her a moment—it will please her so much.

HOLMES - (at door) My dear fellow, it will more than please me! (Opens door. Piano heard off when the door is opened.) Mrs. Watson! Home! Love! Life! Ah, Watson! (Eyes glance about thinking. He sighs a little absently, suddenly turns and goes out.)

(WATSON turns and goes to his desk—not to sit. Enter PARSONS.)

PARSONS - A lady sir, wants to know if she can speak to you. If there's anyone 'ere she won't come in.

WATSON - Any-name?

PARSONS - No, sir. I asked her and she said it was unnecessary—as you wouldn't know 'er. She 'as 'er maid with 'er, sir.

WATSON - Then it must be—Show her in.

(PARSONS turns to go.)

And Parsons—(PARSONS stops and turns.)

(Lower voice.) Two gentlemen, Count von Stalburg and Sir Edward Leighton will call. Bring them here to this room at once, and then tell Mr. Holmes. You'll find him in my dressing-room.

PARSONS - Yes, sir.

WATSON - Send everybody else away—I'll see that lady.

PARSONS - Yes, sir.

(He goes, leaving door open. Brief pause. PARSONS appears outside door, showing some one to the room. Enter ALICE FAULKNER. ALICE glances apprehensively about, fearing she will see HOLMES. Seeing that WATSON is alone, she is much relieved and goes towards him. PARSONS closes door from outside.)

ALICE - (with some timidity) Is this—is this Doctor Watson's room?

WATSON - (encouragingly—and advancing a step or two) Yes, and I am Doctor Watson.

ALICE - Is—would you mind telling me if Mr. Holmes—Mr. —Sherlock Holmes—is here?

WATSON - He will be before long, Miss—er—

ALICE - My name is Alice Faulkner.

WATSON - Miss Faulkner. He came a short time ago, but has gone upstairs for a few moments.

ALICE - Oh!—(with an apprehensive look)—and is he coming down—soon?

WATSON - Well the fact is Miss Faulkner he has an appointment with two gentlemen here and I was to let him know as soon as they arrived.

ALICE - Do you suppose I could wait—without troubling you too much —and see him—afterwards?

WATSON - Why certainly.

ALICE - Thank you—and I—I don't want him to know – that—I—that I came.

WATSON - Of course, if you wish, there's no need of my telling him.

ALICE - It's—very important indeed that you don't, Dr Watson. I can explain it all to you afterwards.

WATSON - No explanation is necessary Miss Faulkner.

ALICE - Thank you (Glances about) I suppose there is a waiting room for patients?

WATSON - Yes or you could sit in there (Indicating surgery door) You'll be less likely to be disturbed.

ALICE - Yes, thank you. (ALICE glances toward door.) I think I would rather be—where its entirely quiet.

(Bell of front door outside rings)

WATSON - (going to surgery door) Then step this way. I think the gentlemen have arrived.

ALICE - (goes to door and turns) And when the business between the gentlemen is over would you please have some one tell me?

WATSON - I'll tell you myself Miss Faulkner.

ALICE - Thank you (She goes)

(PARSONS enters)

PARSONS - Count von Stalburg. Sir Edward Leighton.

(Enter SIR EDWARD and COUNT VON STALBURG. PARSONS goes, closing door after him)

WATSON - Count—Sir Edward—(Bowing and coming forward)

SIR EDWARD - Dr Watson (Bows) Good evening (Placing hat on pedestal.)

(VON STALBURG bows slightly and stands)

Our appointment with Mr. Holmes was changed to your house, I believe

WATSON - Quite right, Sir Edward. Pray be seated, gentlemen.

(SIR EDWARD and WATSON sit.)

VON STALBURG - Mr. Holmes is a trifle late. (Sits.)

WATSON - He has already arrived, Count. I have sent for him.

VON STALBURG - Ugh!

(Slight pause.)

SIR EDWARD - It was quite a surprise to receive his message an hour ago changing the place of meeting. We should otherwise have gone to his house in Baker Street.

WATSON - You would have found it in ashes, Sir Edward.

SIR EDWARD - What! Really!

VON STALBURG - Ugh!

(Both looking at WATSON.)

SIR EDWARD - The—the house burnt!

WATSON - Burning now, probably.

SIR EDWARD - I'm very sorry to hear this. It must be a severe blow to him.

WATSON - No, he minds it very little.

SIR EDWARD - (surprised) Really! I should hardly have thought it.

VON STALBURG - Did I understand you to say, doctor, that you had sent for Mr. Holmes?

WATSON - Yes, Count, and he'll be here shortly. Indeed, I think I hear him on the stairs now.

(Pause. Enter HOLMES at centre door. He is very pale. His clothing is re- arranged and cleansed, though he still, of course, wears the clerical suit, white tie, etc. He stands near door a moment. SIR EDWARD and COUNT rise and turn to him. WATSON rises and goes to desk, where he soon seats himself in chair behind desk. SIR EDWARD and the COUNT stand looking at HOLMES. Brief Pause.)

HOLMES - (coming forward and speaking in a low clear voice, entirely calm, but showing some suppressed feeling or anxiety at the back of it) Gentlemen, be seated again, I beg.

(Brief pause. SIR EDWARD and the COUNT reseat themselves. HOLMES remains standing. He stands looking down before him for quite a while, others looking at him. He finally begins to speak in a low voice without first looking up)

Our business to-night can be quickly disposed of. I need not tell you, gentlemen—for I have already told you—that the part I play in it is more than painful to me. But business is business—and the sooner it is over the better. You were notified to come here this evening in order that I might— (pause)—deliver into your hands the packet which you engaged me—on behalf of your exalted client—

(COUNT and SIR EDWARD bow slightly at "exalted client.")

—to recover. Let me say, in justice to myself, that but for that agreement on my part, and the consequent steps which you took upon the basis of it, I would never have continued with the work. As it was, however, I felt bound to do so, and therefore pursued the matter—to the very end —and I now have the honor to deliver it into your hands.

(HOLMES goes toward SIR EDWARD with the packet. SIR EDWARD rises and meets him. HOLMES places the packet in his hands, COUNT VON STALBURG rises and stands at his chair.)

SIR EDWARD - (formally) Permit me to congratulate you, Holmes, upon the marvellous skill you have displayed, and the promptness with which you have fulfilled your agreement.

(HOLMES bows slightly and turns away. SIR EDWARD at once breaks the seals of the packet and looks at the contents. He begins to show some surprise as he glances at one or two letters or papers and at once looks closer. He quickly motions to COUNT, who goes at once to him. He whispers something to him, and they both look at two or three things together.) ,

VON STALBURG - Oh! No! No!

SIR EDWARD - (stopping examination and looking across to HOLMES) What does this mean? (Pause.)

(HOLMES turns to SIR EDWARD in apparent surprise.)

These letters! And these—other things. Where did you get them?

HOLMES - I purchased them—last night.

SIR EDWARD - Purchased them?

HOLMES - Quite so—quite so.

VON STALBURG - From whom—if I may ask?

HOLMES - From whom? From the parties interested—by consent of Miss Faulkner.

SIR EDWARD - You have been deceived.

HOLMES - What!

(WATSON rises and stands at his desk.)

SIR EDWARD - (excitedly) This packet contains nothing—not a single letter or paper that we wanted. All clever imitations! The photographs are of another person! You have been duped. With all your supposed cleverness, they have tricked you! Ha! ha! ha!

VON STALBURG - Most decidedly duped, Mr. Holmes!

(HOLMES turns quickly to SIR EDWARD.)

HOLMES - Why, this is terrible! (Turns back to WATSON. Stands looking in his face.)

SIR EDWARD - (astonished) Terrible! Surely, sir, you do not mean by that, that there is a possibility you may not be able to recover them!

(Enter ALICE and stands listening.)

HOLMES - It's quite true!

SIR EDWARD - After your positive assurance! After the steps we have taken in the matter by your advice! Why—why, this is—(Turns to COUNT, too indignant to speak.)

VON STALBURG - (indignantly) Surely, sir, you don't mean there is no hope of it?

HOLMES - None whatever, Count. It is too late now! I can't begin all over again!

SIR EDWARD - Why, this is scandalous! It is criminal, sir! You had no right to mislead us in this way, and you shall certainly suffer the consequences. I shall see that you are brought into court to answer for it, Mr. Holmes. It will be such a blow to your reputation that you—

HOLMES - There is nothing to do, Sir Edward—I am ruined – ruined—

ALICE - (coming forward) He is not ruined, Sir Edward. (quiet voice, perfectly calm and self-possessed; she draws the genuine packet from her dress.) It is entirely owing to him and what he said to me that I now wish to give you the—(Starting toward SIR EDWARD as if to hand him the packet.)

(HOLMES steps forward and intercepts her with left hand extended. She stops surprised.)

HOLMES - One moment—(Pause.) Allow me. (He takes packet from her hand.)

(WATSON stands looking at the scene. Pause. HOLMES stands with the package in his hand looking down for a moment. He raises his head, as if he overcame weakness—glances at his watch, and turns to SIR EDWARD and the COUNT. He speaks quietly as if the climax of the tragedy were passed —the deed done. ALICE'S questioning gaze he plainly avoids.)

Gentlemen—(putting watch back in pocket)—I notified you in my letter of this morning that the package should be produced at a quarter-past nine. It is barely fourteen past—and this is it. The one you have there, as you have already discovered, is a counterfeit.

(Love music.)

(HOLMES turns a little, sees ALICE, stands looking at her. ALICE is looking at HOLMES with astonishment and horror. She moves back a little involuntarily.)

SIR EDWARD and VON STALBURG - (staring up with admiration and delight as they perceive the trick) Ah! excellent! Admirable, Mr. Holmes! It is all clear now! Really marvellous! (To one another, etc.) Yes—upon my word!

(On SIR EDWARD and COUNT breaking into expressions of admiration, WATSON quickly moves up to them, and stops them with a quick "Sh!" All stand motionless. HOLMES and ALICE looking at one another. HOLMES goes quickly to ALICE and puts the package into her hands.)

HOLMES - (as he does this) Take this, Miss Faulkner. Take it away from me, quick! It is yours. Never give it up. Use it only for what you wish!

(Stop music.)

SIR EDWARD - (springing forward with a mild exclamation) What! We are not to have it? (Throwing other package up stage.)

(VON STALBURG gives an exclamation or look with foregoing.)

HOLMES - (turning from ALICE—but keeping left hand back upon her hands into which he put the package—as if to make her keep it. Strong —breathless—not loud—with emphatic shake of head) No, you are not to have it.

SIR EDWARD - After all this?

HOLMES - After all this.

VON STALBURG - But, my dear sir—

SIR EDWARD - This is outrageous! Your agreement?

HOLMES - I break it! Do what you please—warrants—summons —arrests—will find me here! (Turns up and says under his breath to WATSON.) Get them out! Get them away! (Stands by WATSON'S desk, his back to the audience.)

(Brief pause. WATSON moves toward SIR EDWARD and the COUNT at the back of HOLMES.)

WATSON - I'm sure, gentlemen, that you will appreciate the fact –

ALICE - (stepping forward—interrupting) Wait a moment, Doctor Watson! (Going to SIR EDWARD.) Here is the package, Sir Edward! (Hands it to SIR EDWARD at once.)

(WATSON motions to PARSONS, off to come on.)

HOLMES - (turning to ALICE) No!

ALICE - (to HOLMES) Yes—(Turning to HOLMES. Pause.) I much prefer that he should have them. Since you last came that night and asked me to give them to you, I have thought of what you said. You were right —it was revenge. (She looks down a moment, then suddenly turns away.)

(HOLMES stands motionless, near corner of desk, his eyes down. PARSONS enters and stands waiting with SIR EDWARD'S hat in his hand, which he took from off pedestal.)

SIR EDWARD - We are greatly indebted to you, Miss Faulkner—

(Looks at VON STALBURG.)

VON STALBURG - To be sure!

SIR EDWARD - And to you, too, Mr. Holmes—if this was a part of the game. (Motionless pause all round. Examining papers carefully. COUNT looking at them also.) It was certainly an extraordinary method of obtaining possession of valuable papers—but we won't quarrel with the method as long as it accomplished the desired result! Eh, Count? (Placing package in breast pocket and buttoning coat.)

VON STALBURG - Certainly not, Sir Edward.

SIR EDWARD - (turning to HOLMES) You have only to notify me of the charge for your services—
(ALICE gives a little look of bitterness at the word "charge")—Mr. Holmes, and you will receive a
cheque I have the honour to wish you—good night.

(Music till end of Act)

(Bowing punctiliously.) Dr. Watson. (Bowing at WATSON.) This way, Count.

(WATSON bows and follows them to door. HOLMES does not move. COUNT VON STALBURG bows to
HOLMES and to WATSON and goes, followed by SIR EDWARD. PARSONS exits after giving SIR
EDWARD his hat. WATSON quietly turns and sees HOLMES beckoning to him. WATSON goes to
HOLMES, who whispers to him after which he quietly goes. HOLMES after a moment's pause, looks
at ALICE.)

HOLMES - (speaks hurriedly) Now that you think it over, Miss Faulkner, you are doubtless beginning
to realize the series of tricks by which I sought to deprive you of your property. I couldn't take it out
of the house that night like a straightforward thief—because it could have been recovered at law,
and for that reason I resorted to a cruel and cowardly device which should induce you to relinquish
it.

ALICE - (not looking at him) But you—you did not give it to them—

(Pause.)

HOLMES - (in a forced cynical hard voice) No—I preferred that you should do as you did.

(ALICE looks suddenly up at him in surprise and pain, with a breathless "What?" scarcely audible.
HOLMES meets her look without a tremor.)

(Slowly, distinctly.) You see, Miss Faulkner, it was a trick —a deception—to the very—end.

(ALICE looks in his face a moment longer and then down.)

Your maid is waiting.

ALICE - (stopping him by speech—no action) And was it —a trick last night—when they tried to kill
you?

HOLMES - (hearing ALICE, stops dead) I went there to purchase the counterfeit package—to use as
you have seen.

ALICE - And—did you know I would come?

(Pause.)

HOLMES - No.

(ALICE gives a subdued breath of relief)

But it fell in with my plans notwithstanding. Now that you see me in my true light, Miss Faulkner, we have nothing left to say but good night – and good-bye—which you ought to be very glad to do. Believe me, I meant no harm to you—it was purely business—with me. For that you see I would sacrifice everything. Even my supposed—friendship for you—was a pretense—a sham—everything that you—

(She has slowly turned away to the front during his speech. She turns and looks him in the face.)

ALICE - (quietly but distinctly) I don't believe it.

(They look at one another.)

HOLMES - (after a while) Why not?

ALICE - From the way you speak—from the way you—look —from all sorts of things!—(With a very slight smile.) You're not the only one—who can tell things—from small details.

HOLMES - (coming a step closer to her) Your faculty—of observation is—is somewhat remarkable, Miss Faulkner—and your deduction is quite correct! I suppose—indeed I know—that I love you. I love you. But I know as well what I am—and what you are –

(ALICE begins to draw nearer to him gradually, but with her face turned front.)

I know that no such person as I should ever dream of being a part of your sweet life! It would be a crime for me to think of such a thing! There is every reason why I should say good-bye and farewell! There is every reason—

(ALICE gently places her right hand on HOLMES' breast, which stops him from continuing speech. He suddenly stops. After an instant he begins slowly to look down into her face. His left arm gradually steals about her. He presses her head close to him and the lights fade away with ALICE resting in HOLMES' arms, her head on his breast.)

(Music swells gradually.)

CURTAIN

Arthur Conan Doyle - A Short Biography

The Scottish physician and writer Sir Arthur Ignatius Conan Doyle's name is inseparable from the phenomenon of Sherlock Holmes, undoubtedly his greatest character and the eponymous meticulous, deductive and frankly genius hero of crime fiction. However, his prolific writing was in more than just the crime fiction genre; alongside the 56 short stories and 4 novels of Sherlock Holmes he explored science fiction and fantasy as well as plays, historical novels and poetry. Another of Conan Doyle's notable characters is Professor Challenger, whose aggression and dominance serves as the antithesis of Holmes, and demonstrates Conan Doyle's capacious imagination and dramatic skill. Returning to his name, it is worthy of note that there is uncertainty surrounding his surname; while he is often referred to as Conan Doyle, where Conan and Doyle are treated as a compound surname, the entry at his baptism records Arthur Ignatius Conan as first names, and Doyle as a solitary last. Indeed, his father's name was simply Doyle. Moreover, the catalogues of the British Library and the Library of Congress insist of Doyle as his surname. Regardless, he began to refer to himself as Conan Doyle and his second wife would take this as her surname, so he will herein be referred to as Conan Doyle, in accordance with his apparent preference.

He was born in Edinburgh at 11 Picardy Place on 22nd May 1859 to his parents Charles Altamont Doyle, an Englishman of Irish descent, and Mary (née Foley), an Irishwoman, who had married in 1855. He had a brother named Innes. Charles was developing an alcohol dependence which would become incompatible with family life, and they dispersed in 1864 at which point the children were temporarily housed at various addresses across Edinburgh. They reunited in 1867, only to live together at 3 Sciennes place in a squalid tenement flat. Fortunately for the children, they had wealthy uncles who were willing to support them by paying for education and clothing. Accordingly at the age of nine Conan Doyle was sent to Hodder Place, Stonyhurst, a Roman Catholic Jesuit preparatory school. He was here for the two years between 1868 and 1870 at which point he went on to Stonyhurst College where he stayed until 1875 when he went for a year to Stella Matutina, Jesuit school in Feldkirch, Austria.

This school education set him up for a place at the University of Edinburgh, where he studied medicine between 1876 and 1881. Part of his course involved placements in Aston, (now a suburb of Birmingham, though at the time it was its own town), Sheffield and in Ruyton-XI-Towns, an unusually named village in Shropshire which acquired its numeral when, in the twelfth century, a castle was built there which became the focus of eleven small and disparate communities. It was during this study that he began writing short stories, with the successful submission of 'The Haunted Grange of Goresthorpe' to Blackwood's Magazine arguably his greatest literary achievement at the time. As well as this recognition, he saw his first published piece 'The Mystery of the Sasassa Valley', a story set in South Africa, printed on 6th September 1879 in Chambers's Edinburgh Journal, and only 17 days later his first non-fiction article was published in the British Medical Journal on 20th September, entitled 'Gelsemium as poison'. Having finished his studies he took an appointment as a Doctor on the Greenland whaler Hope of Peterhead in 1880 and then, following his graduation, he assumed the role of ship's surgeon on the SS Mayumba during its 1881 voyage to the West African coast.

1882 saw his move to Plymouth where he joined the medical practice of former classmate George Turnavine Budd, though they had a difficult professional relationship and Conan Doyle left shortly thereafter in order to set up his own independent practice. Having arrived in Portsmouth in June of that year and disembarked the SS Mayumba with a mere £10 (£700 today) to his name, he proceeded to establish his practice at 1 Bush Billas in Elm Grove, Southsea, a seaside town in the country of Hampshire. He was not met with initial success, and in order to pass the time between visits from patients he resumed his story writing. During this period he completed his first novel, The Mystery of Cloomber, though it was not published until 1888, and the unfinished Narrative of John Smith, which only recently saw publication in 2011. Alongside these longer works was the steady production of a portfolio of short stories which included 'The Captain of the Pole-Star' and 'J. Habakuk Jephson's Statement', both inspired by the time he spent at sea. Meanwhile, in 1885 he completed a doctorate on the subject of tabes dorsalis, the slow degradation and demyelination of the sensory neurons that carry afferent information. He also married Louisa Hawkins, who was the sister of one of his patients, that same year. However, two years after this marriage he met and fell in love with Jean Elizabeth Leckie, though he maintained a platonic relationship with her out of respect for and loyalty to his wife for whom he still had great affection.

Though he struggled to find a publisher for the stories he wrote in these stretches of inactivity, his literary career would take an historic turn in 1886 when, on 20th November, Ward Lock & Co offered Conan Doyle £25 for all rights to A Study In Scarlet. The first and one of the most famous of the Sherlock Holmes franchise, it introduced the public to a new, empirical and methodical mode of crime fiction, and indeed criminality itself, by the combination of a perspicacious, brilliantly observant and data-driven detective whose army doctor companion Watson provided further scientific support as well as a means of observing and narrating Holmes's processes and adventures. The novel was a success; a letter from Robert Louis Stevenson who had acquired a copy of the novel in Samoa, wrote with "[his] compliments on your very ingenious very interesting adventures of Sherlock Holmes", while noting the similarity between Holmes's methods and a certain Joseph Bell, upon whom Holmes was based. Conan Doyle even wrote to Bell explaining so, and that "round the centre of deduction and inference and observation which I have heard you inculcate I have tried to build up a man". It was met with positive reviews in The Scotsman and The Herald and this success encouraged Ward Lock & Co to commission a sequel, The Sign of Four, which appeared in Lippincott's Magazine in February 1890, under agreement with the Ward Lock company. On 28th January 1889 his first child was born, Mary Louise, and three years later on 15th November 1892 they had a boy, Arthur Alleyne Kingsley, who became known only as Kingsley.

Now that he had a family to look after, he began to look more closely at the arrangement he had with his publishers and Conan Doyle soon began to feel that, as a new, inexperienced writer, he had been somewhat exploited by them, resolving to curtail his involvement with their business and instead beginning to write for the Strand Magazine from his home at 2 Wimpole Street. Meanwhile Conan Doyle was enjoying something of a sporting career, playing under the pseudonym A.C. Smith as goalkeeper for Portsmouth Association Football Club (though this club had no connection to present-day Portsmouth F.C, founded two years after Conan Doyle's amateur side disbanded in 1896). He was also a keen cricketer and played ten first-class matches between 1899 and 1907 for the Marylebone Cricket Club, making a highest score with the bat of 43 against London County. As an occasional bowler he only took one wicket in these ten matches, though it was W.G. Grace's stumps which he hit; a notable triumph of the right arm. His sporting interests extended to golf, for which he was elected captain of the Crowborough Beacon Golf Club in East Sussex for 1910. He once even visited Rudyard Kipling at his farm in America, bringing with him a set of golf clubs and giving his fellow famous writer an extended two-day lesson.

He went to Vienna to study ophthalmology in 1890 before returning to London and setting up a practice as an ophthalmologist, though he recorded in his autobiography that not a single patient ever crossed his doorway. This left him with more time for his writing, though by now he was beginning to feel somewhat exhausted by Holmes and wrote to his mother in 1891 "I think of slaying Holmes ... and winding him up for good and all. He takes my mind from better things." This was met with an entreaty from his mother of "you won't! You can't! You mustn't!" These "better things" were his historical novels such as The White Company (1891) and The Great Shadow (1892). Then, in defiance of his mother and the wishes of the general public, in December 1893 he wrote Holmes's apparent death in the clutches of a high-consequence brawl with arch-nemesis Moriarty above the Reichenbach Falls in Germany. Both of their deaths seemed certain, and it seemed the end of the Sherlock Holmes phenomenon. He now had time to focus on other work, most notably his pamphlet justifying the United Kingdom's involvement with the Boer War, an involvement for which they were frequently and heavily criticised. The War in South Africa: Its Cause and Conduct was widely translated after its publication in 1902, and was based to a certain extent on the time he had spent as a volunteer doctor in the Langman Field Hospital at Bloemfontein between March and June 1900. It was this and his book The Great Boer War, written in 1900, which he considered the reasons for his knighthood in 1902 by King Edward VII, and he was subsequently appointed Deputy-Lieutenant of Surrey. In 1903 however, owing to the public demand of which he became increasingly aware after successive letters from fans pleading for the resurrection of their great hero, he seemingly brought Holmes back from the dead; in 'The Adventure of the Empty House', the first story for ten years, he reassures the reader that Holmes had merely arranged for his fall to appear fatal in order that his other enemies (particularly Colonel Sebastian Moran) might consider him dead also, whereas in reality he never falls at all. Fans were ecstatic and Conan Doyle continued to write Holmes stories.

His interest in politics piqued by the issues surrounding the Boer War, the interest he had in criminal justice which was so prominent in his crime fiction transferred to that of real-life and he became a fervent advocate of justice, investigating two closed cases of incorrect conviction. The first, in 1906, saw the shy half-British, half- Indian lawyer George Edalji exonerated for imprisonment for crimes of mutilation towards animals which he hadn't committed. Though the police were convinced of their prosecution, the crimes continued even after he was imprisoned and Conan Doyle, analytical and methodical as his invention, proceeded to privately investigate the case and the outcome, Edalji's acquittal, encouraged the establishment of the Court of Criminal Appeal in 1907. Meanwhile his wife Louisa had been suffering from tuberculosis and died on the 4th July, and Conan Doyle married Jean Elizabeth Leckie, the woman with whom he had fallen in love in 1897, the year after. The second case of injustice was some twenty years later, though pertaining to a crime committed in 1908 allegedly by one Oscar Slater, a German Jew and gambling-den operator convicted of bludgeoning an 82 year old woman to death. Conan Doyle noticed inconsistencies in the evidence which, combined with his general sense of unease about the case, motivated him to pay for the majority of Slater's legal fees and eventually see him released in 1928.

He now had his first child with Jean, whom they named Denis Percy Stewart and was born on 17th March 1909, and then on 19th November 1910 they had Adrian Malcolm. Jean Lena Annette followed on 21st December 1912. Over the next few years there would be various deaths in his family. His first wife having already passed away, Kingsley was taken ill after complications of pneumonia following injury near the Somme in 1917. His two brothers-in-law also died, and after Kingsley's condition worsened and he passed away on 28th October owing to the complications of his convalescence and his brother Innes, now Brigadier-General died of the same, Conan Doyle sank into a deep depression, eventually finding solace in Christian spiritualism. Despite the veracity of his writing, he was not free from misunderstanding. Convinced of the authenticity of five (now known to be) hoaxed photographs of fairies by Elsie Wright in June 1917, he wrote a book The Coming of the Fairies in 1921 exploring them and other supernatural phenomena, followed up in 1926 by The History of Spiritualism, a broader look at the particulars of the movement. Encouraging the Spiritualists' National Union to modify their precepts, his turn to spiritualism was so strong that he wrote a Professor Challenger novel on the subject, entitled The Land of Mist, in 1926.

His friendship with Harry Houdini, another noted Spiritualist, led him to believe that Houdini was possessed of supernatural powers and that his feats were not tricks but proof of the supernatural. He expresses this view in The Edge of the Unknown (1930), and Houdini's inability to convince Conan Doyle of the illusory nature of his feats led to a bitter and very public falling-out. Conan Doyle has been posthumously implicated in the Piltdown Man hoax (and even accused of being its perpetrator by Richard Milner), a discovery of fossilised hominid remains which fooled the scientific world for over 40 years. Milner posits that Conan Doyle's motive was revenge on the scientific establishment for their debunking of Houdini, and that within The Lost World which was released the year the remains were found contains several hidden and encrypted clues indicating his involvement.

On 7th July 1930 Conan Doyle was discovered in the hall of Windlesham Manor, his house in Crowborough, East Sussex, clutching his chest. He died of a heart attack at the age of 71, and his last words, directed to his wife, were "you are wonderful". As a Spiritualist, his burial brought controversy as there was debate as to where he should properly be buried. Eventually he was interred on 11th July in Windlesham rose garden, though he was later removed and buried with his wife in Minstead churchyard in the New Forest, Hampshire.

The epitaph on that gravestone reads

Steel true
Blade straight
Arthur Conan Doyle
Knight
Patriot, Physician and man of letters

Arthur Conan Doyle - A Concise Bibliography

Periodical Publications

Title	Published On	Published In
"The Mystery of the Sasassa Valley"	October 1879	Chambers's Journal
"Gelseminum as a poison"	20 September 1879	British Medical Journal
"The American's Tale"	1879	London Society
"The Gully of Bluemansdyke"	1881	London Society
"Bones"	1882	London Society
"My Friend the Murderer"	1882	London Society
"J. Habakuk Jephson's Statement"	January 1884	Cornhill Magazine
"Life and Death in the Blood"	1884	Good Wordse
"Crabbe's Practice"	1884	The Boy's Own Paper
"The Fate of the Evangeline"	1885	The Boy's Own Paper
"A Psychologist's Wife"	1885	Blackwood's Magazine
"A Midshipman's Story"	December 1885	Cassell's Magazine
"Cyprian Overbeck Wells, or A Literary Mosaic"	1886	The Boy's Own Paper
"Uncle Jeremy's Household"	1887	The Boy's Own Paper
"The Stone of Boxman's Drift"	1887	The Boy's Own Paper
"An Exciting Christmas Eve"	1887	The Boy's Own Paper
"John Huxford's Hiatus"	June 1888	Cornhill Magazine
"The Geographical Distribution of British Intellect"	August 1888	The Nineteenth Century
"The Bravoes of Market Drayton"	August 1889	Chambers's Journal

"The Ring of Thoth"	January 1890	Cornhill Magazine
"The Surgeon of Gaster Fell"	December 1890	Chambers's Journal
"The Duello in France"	December 1890	Cornhill Magazine
"The White Company"	Jan –Dec 1891	Cornhill Magazine
"The Voice of Science"	March 1891	The Strand Magazine
"A Scandal in Bohemia"	July 1891	The Strand Magazine
"The Red-Headed League"	August 1891	The Strand Magazine
"A Case of Identity"	September 1891	The Strand Magazine
"The Boscombe Valley Mystery"	October 1891	The Strand Magazine
"The Five Orange Pips"	November 1891	The Strand Magazine
"The Man with the Twisted Lip"	December 1891	The Strand Magazine
"The Adventure of the Blue Carbuncle"	January 1892	The Strand Magazine
"The Adventure of the Speckled Band"	February 1892	The Strand Magazine
"The Adventure of the Engineer's Thumb"	March 1892	The Strand Magazine
"The Adventure of the Noble Bachelor"	April 1892	The Strand Magazine
"The Adventure of the Beryl Coronet"	May 1892	The Strand Magazine
"The Adventure of the Copper Beeches"	June 1892	The Strand Magazine
"A Day with Dr Conan Doyle"	August 1892	The Strand Magazine
"The Adventure of Silver Blaze"	December 1892	The Strand Magazine
"The Refugees"	January – June 1893	Harper's Magazine
"The Adventure of the Cardboard Box"	January 1893	The Strand Magazine
"The Adventure of the Yellow Face"	February 1893	The Strand Magazine
"The Adventure of the Stockbroker's Clerk"	March 1893	The Strand Magazine
"The Adventure of the Gloria Scott"	April 1893	The Strand Magazine
"The Adventure of the Musgrave Ritual"	May 1893	The Strand Magazine
"The Adventure of the Reigate Squire"	June 1893	The Strand Magazine
"The Green Flag"	June 1893	The Pall Mall Magazine
"The Adventure of the Crooked Man"	July 1893	The Strand Magazine
"The Adventure of the Resident Patient"	August 1893	The Strand Magazine
"Pennarby Mine"	August 1893	The Pall Mall Magazine
"The Adventure of the Greek Interpreter"	September 1893	The Strand Magazine
"The Adventure of the Naval Treaty"	Oct – Nov 1893	The Strand Magazine
"The Adventure of the Final Problem"	December 1893	The Strand Magazine
"The Stark Munro Letters"	1894–1895	The Idler
"The Lord of Chateau Noir"	July 1894	The Strand Magazine
"The Medal of Brigadier Gerard"	December 1894	The Strand Magazine
"The Alpine Pass on Ski"	December 1894	The Strand Magazine
"How the Brigadier Held the King"	April 1895	The Strand Magazine
"How the King Held the Brigadier"	May 1895	The Strand Magazine
"How the Brigadier Slew the Brothers of Ajaccio"	June 1895	The Strand Magazine
"How the Brigadier Came to the Castle of Gloom"	July 1895	The Strand Magazine
"How the Brigadier Took the Field Against the Marshal Millefleurs"	Aug 1895	The Strand Magazine
"How the Brigadier was Tempted by the Devil"	Sept 1895	The Strand Magazine
"How the Brigadier Played for a Kingdom"	December 1895	The Strand Magazine
"Rodney Stone"	Jan – Dec 1896	The Strand Magazine
"The Debut of Bombashi Joyce"	January 1897	Punch
"The Life on a Greenland Whaler"	January – June 1897	The Strand Magazine
"Uncle Barnac"	January – March 1897	The Queen
"The Tragedy of the Korosko"	May – December 1897	The Strand Magazine
"Cremona"	January 1898	Cornhill Magazine
"The Groom's Story"	April 1898	Cornhill Magazine
"The Story of the Beetle Hunter"	June 1898	The Strand Magazine
"The Story of the Man With the Watches"	July 1898	The Strand Magazine
"The Story of the Lost Special"	August 1898	The Strand Magazine
"The Story of the Sealed Room"	September 1898	The Strand Magazine
"The Story of the Black Doctor"	October 1898	The Strand Magazine
"The Story of the Club-Footed Grocer"	November 1898	The Strand Magazine

Title	Date	Magazine
"The Story of the Brazilian Cat"	December 1898	The Strand Magazine
"The Story of the Japanned Box"	January 1899	The Strand Magazine
"The Story of the Jew's Breast-Plate"	February 1899	The Strand Magazine
"The Story of B.24"	March 1899	The Strand Magazine
"The Story of the Latin Tutor"	April 1899	The Strand Magazine
"The Story of the Brown Hand"	May 1899	The Strand Magazine
"The Croxley Master"	Oct – Dec 1899	The Strand Magazine
"The Crime of the Brigadier"	January 1900	The Strand Magazine
"Hilda Wade, 11"	January 1900	The Strand Magazine
"Hilda Wade, 12"	February 1900	The Strand Magazine
"Playing with Fire"	March 1900	The Strand Magazine
"A Glimpse of the Army"	September 1900	The Strand Magazine
"Some Military Lessons of the War"	October 1900	Cornhill Magazine
"The Military Lessons of the War, a Rejoinder"	January 1901	Cornhill Magazine
"The Holocaust of Manor Place"	March 1901	The Strand Magazine
"The Love Affair of George Vincent Parker"	April 1901	The Strand Magazine
"The Debatable Case of Mrs Emsley"	May 1901	The Strand Magazine
"A British Commando"	June 1901	The Strand Magazine
"The Hound of the Baskervilles"	Aug 1901 – April 1902	The Strand Magazine
"How Brigadier Gerard Lost an Ear"	August	The Strand Magazine
"How the Brigadier Saved the Army"	November 1902	The Strand Magazine
"How the Brigadier Rose to Minsk"	December 1902	The Strand Magazine
"Brigadier Gerard at Waterloo"	Jan – Feb 1903	The Strand Magazine
"The Brigadier in England"	March 1903	The Strand Magazine
"How the Brigidier Joined the Hussars at Conflans"	April 1903	The Strand Magazine
"How Etienne Gerard Said Goodbye to his Master"	May 1903	The Strand Magazine
"The Leather Funnel"	June 1903	The Strand Magazine
"The Adventure of the Empty House"	October 1903	The Strand Magazine
"The Adventure of the Norwood Builder"	November 1903	The Strand Magazine
"The Adventure of the Dancing Men"	December 1903	The Strand Magazine
"The Adventure of the Solitary Cyclist"	January 1904	The Strand Magazine
"The Adventure of the Priory School"	February 1904	The Strand Magazine
"The Adventure of Black Peter"	March 1904	The Strand Magazine
"The Adventure of Charles Augustus Milverton"	April 1904	The Strand Magazine
"The Adventure of the Six Napoleons"	May 1904	The Strand Magazine
"The Adventure of the Three Students"	June 1904	The Strand Magazine
"The Adventure of the Golden Pince-Nez"	July 1904	The Strand Magazine
"The Adventure of the Missing Three-Quarter"	August 1904	The Strand Magazine
"The Adventure of the Abbey Grange"	September 1904	The Strand Magazine
"The Adventure of the Second Stain"	December 1904	The Strand Magazine
"The Great Brown-Pericord Motor"	January 1905	The Pictorial Magazine
"Sir Nigel"	Dec 1905 – Dec 1906	The Strand Magazine
"An Incusion into Diplomacy"	June 1906	Cornhill Magazine
"Through the Magic Door"	Nov 1906 – Oct 1907	Cassell's Magazine
"The Pot of Caviare"	March 1908	The Strand Magazine
"The Silver Mirror"	August 1908	The Strand Magazine
"The Singular Experience of Mr. John Scott Eccles"	Sept 1908	The Strand Magazine
"The Tiger of San Pedro"	October 1908	The Strand Magazine
"The Adventure of the Bruce-Partington Plans"	December 1908	The Strand Magazine
"Shakespeare's Expostulation"	March 1909	Cornhill Magazine
"Bendy's Sermon"	April 1909	The Strand Magazine
"The Lord of Falcolnbridge"	August 1909	The Strand Magazine
"Some Recollections of Sport"	September 1909	The Strand Magazine
"The Homecoming"	December 1909	The Strand Magazine
"The Terror of Blue John Gap"	August 1910	The Strand Magazine
"The Marriage of the Brigadier"	September 1910	The Strand Magazine
"The Adventure of the Devil's Foot"	December 1910	The Strand Magazine

"The Adventure of the Red Circle"	March – April 1911	The Strand Magazine
"The Giant Maximin"	July 1911	The Literary Pageant
"One Crowded Hour"	August 1911	The Strand Magazine
"What Reform is Needed?"	September 1911	The Strand Magazine
"The Disappearance of Lady Frances Carfax"	December 1911	The Strand Magazine
"The Lost World"	April – Nov 1912	The Strand Magazine
"The Fall of Lord Barrymore"	December 1912	The Strand Magazine
"The Poison Belt"	March – July 1913	The Strand Magazine
"England and the Next War"	1913	The Fortnightly Review
"How it Happened"	September 1913	The Strand Magazine
"The Horror of the Heights"	November 1913	The Strand Magazine
"The Adventure of the Dying Detective"	December 1913	The Strand Magazine
"Essays Upon Phases of the Great War"	1914	The Fortnightly Review
"Danger!"	July 1914	The Strand Magazine
"The Valley of Fear"	Sept 1914 – May 1915	The Strand Magazine
"Western Wanderings"	January – April 1915	Cornhill Magazine
"Sherlock Holmes Drawn by a Typewriter"	August 1915	The Strand Magazine
"An Outing in War Time"	October 1915	The Strand Magazine
"Stranger than Fiction"	December 1915	The Strand Magazine
"The Prisoner's Defence"	February 1916	The Strand Magazine
"The British Campaign in France"	April – June 1917	The Strand Magazine
"Is Sir Oliver Lodge Right that the Dead Can Communicate?"	July 1917	The Strand Magazine
"What Will England be Like in 1930?"	August 1917	The Strand Magazine
"His Last Bow"	September 1917	The Strand Magazine
"Some Personalia about Mr Sherlock Holmes"	December 1917	The Strand Magazine
"Three of Them"	April 1918	The Strand Magazine
"The Battle of the Somme"	May – June 1918	The Strand Magazine
"Three of Them"	July – August 1918	The Strand Magazine
"The British Campaign in France"	Oct – Nov 1918	The Strand Magazine
"Three of Them"	December 1918	The Strand Magazine
"The Battle of Cambrai"	Jan – Feb 1919	The Strand Magazine
"Life After Death"	March 1919	The Strand Magazine
"The Uncharted Coast"	Dec 1919, Jan, May, Sept & Nov 1920	The Strand Magazine
"The Sideric Pendulum"	August 1920	The Strand Magazine
"Faries Photographed"	December 1920	The Strand Magazine
"The Evidence for Faries"	March 1921	The Strand Magazine
"The Uncharted Coast"	May 1921	The Strand Magazine
"Sherlock Holmes on the Film"	July 1921	The Strand Magazine
"The Adventure of the Mazarin Stone"	October 1921	The Strand Magazine
"The Bully of Brocas"	November 1921	The Strand Magazine
"The Nightmare Room"	December 1921	The Strand Magazine
"The Problem of Thor Bridge"	Feb – March 1922	The Strand Magazine
"The Lift"	June 1922	The Strand Magazine
"Now, Then Smith!"	July 1922	The Strand Magazine
"Sherlock Holmes in Real Life"	September 1922	The Strand Magazine
"A Point of Contact"	October 1922	The Story-Teller
"Billy's Bones"	December 1922	The Strand Magazine
"The Centurion"	December 1922	The Story-Teller
"The Cottingley Faries"	February 1923	The Strand Magazine
"The Adventure of the Creeping Man"	March 1923	The Strand Magazine
"Haunting Dreams"	April 1923	The Strand Magazine
"The Forbidden Subject"	August 1923	The Strand Magazine
"Memories and Adventures"	Oct 1923 – July 1924	The Strand Magazine
"How Our Novelists Write Their Books"	December 1924	The Strand Magazine
"The Adventure of the Three Garridebs"	January 1925	The Strand Magazine
"The Adventure of the Illustrious Client"	Feb –March 1925	The Strand Magazine
"The Land of Mist"	July 1925 – March 1926	The Strand Magazine

"The Adventure of the Three Gables"	October 1926	The Strand Magazine
"The Adventure of the Blanched Soldier"	November 1926	The Strand Magazine
"The Adventure of the Lion's Mane"	December 1926	The Strand Magazine
"The Adventure of the Retired Colourman"	January 1927	The Strand Magazine
"The Adventure of the Veiled Lodger"	February 1927	The Strand Magazine
"The Adventure of Shoscombe Old Place"	April 1927	The Strand Magazine
"W.G. Grace—A Memory"	July 1927	The Strand Magazine
"Houdini the Enigma"	August – Sept 1927	The Strand Magazine
"The Maracot Deep"	Oct 1927 – Feb 1928	The Strand Magazine
" When the World Screamed"	April – May 1928	The Strand Magazine
"The Dreamers—Notes from a Strange Mail Bag"	June 1928	The Strand Magazine
"The Story of Spedegue's Dropper"	October 1928	The Strand Magazine
"The Disintegration Machine"	January 1929	The Strand Magazine
"The Lord of the Dark Face"	April – May 1929	The Strand Magazine
"The Death Voyage"	October 1929	The Strand Magazine

Novels

A Study in Scarlet (1887)
Micah Clarke (1889)
The Mystery of Cloomber (1889)
The Sign of the Four (1890)
The Firm of Girdlestone (1890)
The White Company (1891)
The Doings of Raffles Haw (1891)
The Great Shadow (1892)
The Refugees (1893)
The Parasite (1894)
The Stark Munro Letters (1895)
Rodney Stone (1896)
Uncle Bernac (1897)
The Tragedy of the Korosko (1898)
A Duet, with an Occasional Chorus (1899)
The Hound of the Baskervilles (1902)
Sir Nigel (1906)
The Lost World (1912)
The Poison Belt (1913)
The Valley of Fear (1915)
The Land of Mist (1926)
The Maracot Deep (1929) Novel with three short stories

Short Story Collections

Mysteries and Adventures (1890)
The Captain of the Polestar and Other Tales (1890)
The Adventures of Sherlock Holmes (1892)
The Gully of Bluemansdyke (1893)
The Memoirs of Sherlock Holmes (1894)
Round the Red Lamp: Being Facts and Fancies of Medical Life (1894)
The Exploits of Brigadier Gerard (1896)
The Green Flag and Other Stories of War and Sport (1900)
The Adventures of Gerard (1903)
The Return of Sherlock Holmes (1905)
Round the Fire Stories (1908)
The Last Galley (1911)
His Last Bow (1917)
Danger! and Other Stories (1918)

Three of Them (1923)
The Case-Book of Sherlock Holmes (1927)

Stage works of Doyle
Jane Annie; or, The Good Conduct Prize (1893) Libretto to operetta, with J.M. Barrie; music by Ernest Ford
Foreign Policy (1893) Based on A Question of Diplomacy
The Story of Waterloo (1894) A one-act play written for Sir Henry Irving
Brothers (1899) Based on novel Halves by James Payn
Sherlock Holmes (1899) with William Gillette
A Duet (1902)
Brigadier Gerard (1906)
The Fires of Fate (1909)
The House of Temperley (1910)
A Pot of Caviare (1910)
The Speckled Band (1910)
The Crown Diamond (1921)
It's Time Something Happened (1925)
Exile: A Drama of Christmas Eve (1925)
The Journey

Poetry
Songs of Action (1898)
Songs of the Road (1911)
The Guards Came Through, and Other Poems (1919)
The Poems of Arthur Conan Doyle: Collected Edition (1922)

Non Fiction
The Great Boer War (1900)
The War in South Africa – Its Cause and Conduct (1902)
Through the Magic Door (1907)
The Crime of the Congo (1909)
The Case of Oscar Slater (1912)
The German War: Some Sidelights and Reflections (1914)
A Visit to Three Fronts (1916)
The British Campaign in France and Flanders1916–20
Memories and Adventures (1924)

Spiritualist and Paranormal Books
The New Revelation (1918)
The Vital Message (1919)
Verbatim Report of a Public Debate on 'The Truth of Spiritualism' between Sir Arthur Conan Doyle and Joseph McCabe (1920)
The Wanderings of a Spiritualist (1921)
The Coming of the Fairies (1922)
The Case for Spirit Photography (1922)
Our American Adventure (1923)
Our Second American Adventure (1924)
The Spiritualist's Reader (1924)
The History of Spiritualism (1926)
Phineas Speaks (1927)
Our African Winter (1929)
The Edge of the Unknown (1930)

Pamphlets

A Full Report of a Lecture on Spiritualism Delivered by Sir Arthur Conan Doyle at the Connaught Hall, Worthing on Friday July 11th 1919 (1919) 11 pages

Our reply to the Cleric: Sir Arthur Conan Doyle's Lecture in Leicester, October 19th 1919 (1920) 16 pages

Spiritualism and Rationalism (1920) 32 pages

The Early Christian Church and Modern Spiritualism (1925) 12 pages

Psychic Experiences (1925) 12 pages

A Word of Warning (1928) 19 pages

What Does Spiritualism Actually Teach and Stand For? (1928) 16 pages

The Roman Catholic Church: A Rejoinder (1929) 72 pages

An Open Letter to Those of My Generation (1929) 12 pages

The New Revelation (1997) 32 pages

www.ingramcontent.com/pod-product-compliance
Lightning Source LLC
Chambersburg PA
CBHW060117050426
42448CB00010B/1909